ARTICLE V
UNLEASHED

A Citizen's History Of
Constitutional Change

Empowering You To Help Shape
America's Future

John van Compernolle

Article V Unleashed
A Citizen's History Of Constitutional Change

Published by B-Global Publishing.
Copyright © 2023

DEDICATION

We the People of the United States, in Order to form a more perfect Union, establish Justice, ensure domestic Tranquility, provide for the common defense, promote the general Welfare, and secure the **Blessings of Liberty to ourselves and our Posterity**, do ordain and establish this Constitution for the United States of America.

I do solemnly swear that I will support and **defend the Constitution of the United States against all enemies, foreign and domestic**; that I will bear true faith and allegiance to the same; and that I will obey the orders of the President of the United States and the orders of the officers appointed over me, according to regulations and the Uniform Code of Military Justice. So help me God (Title 10, US Code; Act of 5 May 1960 replacing the wording first adopted in 1789, with amendment effective 5 October 1962).

The Blessings of Liberty are a gift that our fore-fathers gave to "ourselves and our posterity". The gift is not free. It requires our vigilance. It requires active participation. It requires that a limited government remains limited.

I joined the Navy and took that oath in 1972 with a foreign enemy in mind. As did my grandfather, John Jackson Loudin - Marine Corp, my father Remi van Compernolle, Jr. – Army Air Corp, my step-son James Edward Mosley – Army Airborne, my son Matthew Richard van Compernolle – Air Force, and most recently, at age 17, my grandson Robert Curtis Mosely – Army Airborne.

That Oath does not expire. Ever. The Constitution which we promised to defend against all enemies, foreign and domestic, has been under attack by a domestic enemy the entire time. Five generations of my family have had a foreign enemy in mind. This book is to show how a domestic enemy has improperly altered the meaning and intent of that limiting document, and how we have, as yet, been unsuccessful in defending it using its built-in defense system, Article V.

This book is dedicated to my son Matt and grandson Curt, that they may not forget their oaths, and that they may know the domestic enemy. Also, to my great-grand-son, Jax Loudin Mosley, whose future liberty we need to ensure. The limits set forth in the original constitution were the vehicle to secure the blessings of liberty. The domestic enemy uses words and courts to soften or eliminate limits on its power. The erosion of those limits necessarily erodes liberty. The foreign enemy may be deterred with ships, planes, and bullets. We must fight the domestic enemy with words, which put those limits back in place, and at full strength.

NOTES TO THE READER:

Dear Reader, do you remember having your essays reviewed by your English teacher and feeling that you have no idea how to write the English language? Well then write a book and have it edited by a true professional and you will relive that experience. Thank you so much to Dr. Randi D. Ward for your professionalism and attention to detail.

I did get a few concessions from her, and to protect her integrity I am compelled to explain here what those concessions were.

First, as you read many of the quoted documents and excerpts from the Congressional Record, you will find many words and phrases not exactly to your liking. I want you to know that Dr. Randi did her very best to correct the spelling and phrases.

Students of founding documents will already know that spelling and phrasing in the 18th century were not the same as today. In the direct copying of the U.S. Constitution, Articles of Confederation, and a few quotes from other older writing you will find those "mis-spellings" and "grammatical errors". They remain in this book at my insistence, and are not the result of any error on the part of Dr. Randi..

Further, the citations given for the references to quotes from the congressional record may look very much like errors themselves. That also may require explanation here. What follows is an example of how to interpret their meaning:

Citation: *(40 Cong. Rec. 4551, 1906)*

40 Cong. Rec. - refers to the record of the 40th Congressional Session. Each Congressional Session covers the two year period between Congressional Elections. Hence, the 40th session followed the elections of 1904, and encompasses the records from 1905 and 1906.

4551 - refers to the page number or numbers on which the quote may be found.

1906 - is the session year from which the quote is taken.

Article V Unleashed

TABLE OF CONTENTS

0

INTRODUCTION

Over the course of 236 years, our Constitution has served to guide our law-makers, protect our God given rights, and in general, place some constraints on the powers of the federal government. However, in the most recent 131 years the federal government has found ways to encroach upon those powers, which had been exclusively reserved for the States or the people. This encroachment has been accomplished by many modes, almost none by actually amending the Constitution to make the extra-constitutional powers being exercised a part of our legal foundation.

Over time, Presidents have declared that they have certain powers not actually in existence and made them stick. Much of this is through the use of the "executive order". Executive orders, when used appropriately, instruct the administration on policy with regard to carrying into force the laws of the nation. After all, the President is to "take care that the laws be faithfully executed". Over the course of time, we have seen executive orders instruct the administration to ignore laws or to take actions which have not been enacted into law, thus making his own law. This seems less than a faithful execution of the law.

Over time, we have seen Congress pass laws which are in clear contradiction of Constitutional prohibitions or laws which have no basis in actual rational thinking to those powers granted to the Congress. These have been accomplished by stretching definitions of plain English words of the Constitution. The most common words stretched are the General Welfare clause and the Commerce clause. To be sure, Congress has not accomplished this alone. It required the complicity of the President to sign such acts into law, and the complicity of the Judiciary to validate the language thus stretched. The complicity of the President and the Judiciary is most commonly found when Congress delegates law-making authority to an agency formed to regulate some aspect of our lives. Some of these agencies are unconstitutional in their very existence, in that they have no basis for that existence in Article I, Section 8, and may even be prohibited from existing in Article I, Section 9. Other agencies may find support for their existence in Article I, but being a part of the Executive branch, they are not empowered with law-making authority. After all, that is the first sentence in Article I, "All legislative powers herein granted shall be vested in a Congress". All, means none can reside elsewhere.

The Judiciary is sometimes complicit and sometimes our savior when it comes to challenges to the less than Constitutional actions of the President, Agencies, or the Congress. From time to time, they stick to the words of the Constitution. More often than not, they are swayed by the stretching of Constitutional words by slick talking lawyers and become complicit in the encroachment. Sometimes, in the self-righteous ways of people in power, they overextend the solution creating an entirely new law, which Congress did not enact, and the President did not sign, but still, it will hold up in the next court case as precedent. On occasion, a new set of Justices will get the opportunity to correct one of these blunders and overturn a precedent, making things a little better than they were. Adherence to precedent is a pillar of our common law system, so most judges are very reticent to overturn a prior decision when they have the opportunity.

With all of this overreaching by the federal powers, what are we the people left to do? That would be the jurisdiction of our state legislatures. They are our protectors, after all, in the words of James Madison in Federalist 85, "We may safely rely on the disposition of the State legislatures to erect barriers against the encroachments of the national authority." But what mode of erecting such barriers are available to these state legislatures? Can they make laws to contradict federal laws? Article VI, Section 2, says no, they cannot; federal laws are superior.

I would suggest to you that the barrier erecting tool is clearly laid out for us in Article V. Article V is a power valve inserted into the Constitution. It allows, on the one hand, Congress to propose an alteration in their powers to be either granted or not by the acceptance of three-quarters of the several states. On the other hand, it also allows for states to propose an alteration in federal powers to be either granted or not by the acceptance of three-quarters of the several states.

At this point, you may be asking why this has not been used by those state legislatures to erect such barriers against the encroachments of the national authority. If you are, then you see that Article V needs to be unleashed.

That is exactly what this book will show you—the struggle of state legislatures to amass the collective political will to unleash Article V to force Congress to do their Constitutionally Mandatory Duty. I will show that these conditions to trigger this Congressional Required Action may have been met constantly from 1907 to this very day. Congress has been in dereliction of that duty. Some people believe that many critics and constitutional scholars are wrong, and the states have not yet met that threshold.

The answer lies in the resolution of two questions.
1) What constitutes an application consistent with Article V?
2) Who has the authority to determine whether the two-thirds threshold has been met?

The Constitution is silent on both of these, thus leaving it to the collective political will of state legislatures to be stronger than the will of Congress. In order for state legislators to amass any political will, they need constituents pressuring them. This is how YOU can help form the future of America.

This book and much of my acquired knowledge as a result of this effort would not have been possible were it not for the existence of the Article V Library.

It can be found at: http://articlevlibrary.com/applications.htm

THE U.S. CONSTITUTION

Since this book is about the history of the use of an Article V Convention to amend the Constitution, understanding the Constitution is a good first step. The complete U.S. Constitution and its 27 amendments are in Appendix I.

Our Constitution establishes a federal government consisting of three branches: the Congress, the Executive, and the Judiciary.

ARTICLE I - THE CONGRESS

Congress has the sole power of creating legislation and is made up of two chambers, the House of Representatives and the Senate. Representatives are elected every two years by the people in their district, and each state has a portion of the 435 members apportioned based on population. A census is taken every ten years, and the number of representatives each state gets is changed based on the new population. The Senate is made up of two senators from each state. Originally, they were appointed by the State Legislature, but the 17th amendment made them elected by the people of the state. Senators serve for six years, with one third coming up for election every two years. The House has the sole power of impeachment, which is making a charge of wrongdoing by an elected or appointed government official. The Senate has the sole power of trying all impeachments, which is the determination of innocence or guilt of the charges made by the House. The Congress is assigned specific powers and duties. Members of Congress are assigned special rights and prohibitions while they are in office. The legislative process requires that bills raising revenues must originate in the House. All bills must pass both the House and the Senate and be signed by the President before becoming law. The President may veto a bill, but the Congress can override the veto with a two-thirds vote in the House and the Senate.

The Congress is granted very specific powers:
1. Lay and collect taxes, duties, imposts, and excises uniformly throughout the United States
2. Pay the debts
3. Provide for the common defense and general welfare

4. Borrow Money
5. Regulate Commerce with Foreign Nations, between the States, and with Indian Tribes
6. Make rules of naturalization
7. Make laws of bankruptcies
8. Coin money, regulate its value and the value of foreign money
9. Maintain a standard of weights and measures
10. Punish counterfeiting securities and money
11. Establish a post office and post roads
12. Provide for copyrights and patents to authors and inventors
13. Establish a federal court system inferior to the Supreme Court
14. Define and punish piracies and felonies on the high seas and against the law of nations
15. Declare war, grant letters of marque and reprisal, and make rules on captures on land and water
16. Raise and support armies but finance them for no longer than two years at a time
17. Maintain a Navy
18. Make rules for the government of land and naval forces
19. Provide for calling the militia to execute federal laws, suppress insurrections, and repel invasions
20. Provide for organizing, arming, and disciplining the militia, governing those in federal service, but the states will appoint officers and train the militia to the discipline prescribed by congress
21. Exercise exclusive legislation over the federal district (District of Columbia) and other locations of federal use such as forts, arsenals, etc.
22. Make laws necessary and proper to accomplish 1-21 above

The Congress is denied any power to:

- Alter the slave trade prior to 1808 (obsolete both in time and purpose)
- Suspend Habeas Corpus except in case of rebellion or invasion
- Issue bills of attainder or ex post facto laws
- Lay taxes directly on people or states out of proportion with the census (removed by the 16th amendment)
- Impose tax or duty on articles exported from any State
- Make preferential regulation of commerce for one State over another

- Impose duties on or oblige vessels to enter or clear one State when entering from another State
- Spend money without specific appropriation made by law and must publish accounting
- Assign title of nobility, and no office holder may accept such or any emoluments from foreign states

States may not execute any of the powers granted to Congress above.

ARTICLE II - THE EXECUTIVE

The executive power shall be vested in a President. Executive power means enforcement of laws and ensuring that the responsibilities of the government are properly executed. The President and a Vice President are elected together for a term of four years by an Electoral College. Originally, the Electors would vote for two people, at least one of which could not reside in their State. The person with the most votes would be President, and the second most would be Vice President. The 12th Amendment changed this so that there was a vote for President and a separate vote for Vice President. In case no one person has a majority, the Congress shall decide by ballot. Each State will have one vote in this case. In case of removal or death of a President, the 25th Amendment completely replaces the original process. The President is paid a salary but cannot receive emoluments from the United States or any State. He must take an oath of office "I do solemnly swear that I will faithfully execute the Office of President of the United States and will to the best of my ability, preserve, protect, and defend the Constitution of the United States." (U.S. Constitution Article 2, Section 1, Clause 7)

The members of the Electoral College, Electors, are appointed as each State Legislature may decide, and each State will have a number of Electors equal to the total number of Representatives and Senators that State is entitled to. Congress decides the day upon which Electors are chosen and the day they must present their votes to Congress. The President of the Senate will open and read the votes in the presence of the Representatives and Senators.

The President has the following powers and duties:
- Commander in Chief of the Army and Navy
- Commander in Chief of the Militia of the several States when called into service
- To require, in writing, the opinion of the officer of each executive department related to the duties of that office
- To grant reprieves and pardons for offenses against the United States, except in cases of impeachment
- To make treaties with the advice and consent of the Senate
- With the advice and consent of the Senate, appoint ambassadors, ministers and consuls, judges of the Supreme Court, and all other officers not provided for elsewhere. But Congress may vest the appointment of inferior offices in the President, Courts, or Department Heads.
- He must from time to time provide Congress with a report on the State of the Union,
- He may recommend such actions as he thinks the Congress should take.
- He may call either or both chambers into session. If both chambers do not agree on a time of adjournment, he may adjourn them till a time he thinks proper.
- He shall receive ambassadors and other public ministers.
- He shall take care that the laws be faithfully executed.
- He shall commission all the officers of the United States.

The President, Vice President, and all civil officers of the United States shall be removed from office on impeachment for, and conviction of, treason, bribery, or other high crimes and misdemeanors.

ARTICLE III - THE JUDICIARY

There will be one Supreme Court and as many inferior federal courts and judges as the Congress shall decide. Federal judges are appointed by the President, confirmed by the Senate, and hold office during good behavior.

Federal court has appellate jurisdiction both as to law and fact in the following:

- Cases and controversies in law and equity under this Constitution
- Treaties made or to be made under their authority
- Cases affecting ambassadors and other public ministers and consuls and of a State, if the State is a party to the case, the federal court will have original jurisdiction
- Cases of admiralty and maritime jurisdiction
- Cases where the United States is a party
- Cases between a State and citizen(s) of another State. (The 11th amendment changes this to exclude cases where the citizen(s) of another State initiated the legal action.)
- Cases between citizens of different States
- Cases between citizens of the same State claiming land under grants of a different State
- Cases between a State or citizens thereof and foreign citizens or subjects

Congress may make exceptions to the above. All trials of crimes, except impeachment, will be by jury and held in the State where the crime is committed.

Treason against the United States consists only in levying war against them or in adhering to the enemies, giving them aid and comfort. Conviction for treason may only proceed if there are two witnesses who testify to the same overt act in open court.

ARTICLE IV – RELATIONSHIP BETWEEN STATES

Every State must give full faith and credit to the acts, records, and judicial proceedings of every other State. Congress will decide how such acts, records, and proceedings shall be proved and the effect they will have.

Citizens of each State are entitled to the privileges and immunities of citizens in the several States. Citizens who flee from criminal prosecution to another state shall be returned by that State for prosecution.

New States may be admitted to the Union. New States may not be formed from part of an existing State or the combination of two States or parts of two States without the consent of the legislatures of the State involved and the Congress. Congress has the power to dispose of and regulate all territory or property belonging to the United States.

The United States will guarantee to every State a Republican form of government. The United States shall protect each State from invasion and when asked by a State legislature or executive against domestic violence.

ARTICLE V – HOW TO AMEND THIS CONSTITUTION

This article provides for two methods of proposing amendments and two methods for ratification of proposed amendments. Because this article is at the center of the history put forward in this book, I'll put the full text of the article here and explain it in simple terms.

Here is the full text of Article V:

The Congress, whenever two thirds of both Houses shall deem it necessary, shall propose Amendments to this Constitution, or, on the Application of the Legislatures of two thirds of the several States, shall call a Convention for proposing Amendments, which, in either Case, shall be valid to all Intents and Purposes, as Part of this Constitution, when ratified by the Legislatures of three fourths of the several States, or by Conventions in three fourths thereof, as the one or the other Mode of Ratification may be proposed by the Congress; Provided that no Amendment which may be made prior to the Year One thousand eight hundred and eight shall in any Manner affect the first and fourth Clauses in the Ninth Section of the first Article; and that no State, without its Consent, shall be deprived of its equal Suffrage in the Senate.

Congress may propose an amendment by a vote of two-thirds on the language of that amendment in both the House and the Senate. That is 290 in the House and 67 in the Senate.

The States may propose an amendment by a convention for that purpose. When two-thirds of State Legislatures, 34, have requested that Congress call a convention, Congress MUST call a convention.

Congress may direct that a proposed amendment be submitted to a vote by the State legislatures for ratification. Three fourths of the States Legislatures, 38, must approve of the proposed amendment for it to take effect.

Congress may direct that a proposed amendment be submitted to a State Convention to be voted on for ratification. Three fourths of the State Conventions, 38, must approve of the proposed amendment for it to take effect.

Once proposed by either method and ratified by either method, an amendment shall be valid as part of this Constitution.

Finally, the obsolete section prevents any amendment altering the counting of three fifths of the slaves in the census to determine the representation in the House prior to 1808, nor the equal representation of each State in the Senate.

ARTICLE VI – EXISTING DEBT, SUPREMACY AND OATHS

All of the debts contracted by the Confederation Congress shall be assumed by the Congress under this Constitution once adopted by the States.

This Constitution and the laws made under its provisions and all treaties made or to be made by the United States shall be the supreme law of the land. Judges in every State shall be bound by this Constitution, laws, and treaties.

All Senators and Representatives, State Legislatures, and Executive and Judicial Officers of the United States and each State shall be bound by an Oath to support this Constitution.

No religious test shall ever be required as a qualification to any office or public trust under the United States.

ARTICLE VII – RATIFICATION OF THIS CONSTITUTION

The ratification of the conventions of nine States shall be sufficient for the establishment of this constitution between the States so ratifying the same.

Once nine States ratify this constitution by vote of a ratifying convention in that state, those nine States become the United States of America, and this Constitution takes effect. The other four States remain independent countries or sovereignties until such time as they ratify this Constitution and join the union.

KEY PRINCIPLES WITHIN THE CONSTITUTION

There are several key principles built into the structure of our Constitution. Part of governing within the Constitution is to keep faith with these principles as much as following the meaning of the words. Each of these principles were, and are, seen as ways to ensure the liberties of a free self-governing people.

First, the **separation of powers**. By having three branches of government, power is disbursed instead of concentrated. In order to control all the power of government would require cooperation between two or all three branches and is, therefore, very difficult if not impossible. The specific powers being separated are the ability to make law, the ability to enforce law, and the ability to adjudicate and punish lawbreakers.

Next are the **checks and balances**. No one branch has full power where it is charged with the primary role. For example, Congress has all law-making authority, but the President may stop a law from becoming effective. The executive may charge and arrest someone for breaking the law but cannot find them guilty and either fine or imprison them. The President may appoint judges, but the Senate may reject them, and Congress cannot appoint them. The federal courts may apply the law to a case or controversy brought before it but may not comment on a law outside of a case or controversy.

There's also the theory of **non-delegation**. This is to say that when the Congress is vested with ALL legislative power, they may not through law or any other means grant that law making authority to any other branch or outside organization. The President has ALL executive powers and may not delegate any of that power to the other branches or outside organization.

The principle of **representation of different constituents** is also built in. The House of Representatives is elected by the people and represents them. The Senate was appointed by the State Legislatures to represent the States, but the 17th Amendment changed that to popular election, and the States are left unrepresented today. The President is elected by the Electoral College but is intended to represent the whole country to the world.

The principle of **shared sovereignty** is very important. Based on the powers granted, the federal government in Article I and II, the States gave up sovereignty on those subjects but retained sovereignty on all other subjects. This means that the federal government cannot make laws on non-delegated subjects which are supreme over any State law or even a lack thereof. The States retain full sovereignty on all powers not specifically delegated to the federal government.

The Constitution did not contain any sort of Bill of Rights, even though that question had been heavily debated. That debate occurred at the convention and in all of the states during the ratification process. However, once the ninth state, New Hampshire, had ratified the Constitution, it now was in full force for those nine states of the United States of America. Virginia and New York ratified during the next month despite heated debates of the Bill of Rights issue, bringing the number of United States to eleven. At this point, the Bill of Rights issue became soluble only by use of Article V of the new Constitution.

RATIFICATION OF THE CONSTITUTION

On September 17, 1787, the Constitution of the United States was accepted by the delegates to the Constitutional Convention. Of the 42 delegates still present at the convention when it was finished, 39 signed the Constitution. Only Governor Edmund Randolph (Virginia), George Mason (Virginia), and Elbridge Gerry (Massachusetts) declined to sign.

The Founding Fathers now had to get the states to agree to the document and to vote in favor of it in state conventions. Nine states needed to vote for the Constitution for it to be accepted. On December 7, 1787, Delaware was the first state to vote in favor of ratification. New Hampshire became the ninth state to accept the Constitution on June 21, 1788, which officially ended government under the Articles of Confederation. It was not until May 29, 1790, that the last state, Rhode Island, finally ratified the Constitution.

The states and the dates of ratification are listed in order of ratification:
1.   **Delaware**: December 7, 1787
2.   **Pennsylvania**: December 12, 1787
3.   **New Jersey**: December 18, 1787
4.   **Georgia**: January 2, 1788
5.   **Connecticut**: January 9, 1788
6.   **Massachusetts**: February 6, 1788
7.   **Maryland**: April 28, 1788
8.   **South Carolina**: May 23, 1788
9.   **New Hampshire**: June 21, 1788 (9TH State)
10.   **Virginia**: June 25, 1788
11.   **New York**: July 26, 1788
12.   **North Carolina**: November 21, 1789
13.   **Rhode Island**: May 29, 1790

ARTICLE V USAGE

When the government, through legislation or unchecked action departs from the principles or the meaning of the words in the Constitution, this results in more concentration of power, fewer checks, and less balance. The founding fathers realized that they could not cover all the bases to keep the government responsive and protective of the people, and that is why they provided a way to add to or change the Constitution. This is in Article V. Near the end of the Constitutional Convention, Article V contained only the provision for Congress to propose amendments.

The Congress, whenever two thirds of both Houses shall deem it necessary, shall propose Amendments to this Constitution....

George Mason realized that the States needed to be able to propose them as well. He realized that Article V should be a valve to allow the Congress to ask for more power through proposed amendments and a way for the States to reduce that power through proposed amendments. Either way, the States or the People through State Conventions become the final decision on any proposed amendment.

... or, on the Application of the Legislatures of two thirds of the several States, shall call a Convention for proposing Amendments....

This suggestion resulted in changes to Article V which the convention agreed to unanimously without debate.

CONGRESS PROPOSED AMENDMENTS

There have been nearly 12,000 attempts by Congress (resolutions filed by members) to propose amendments. Congress has only proposed 33 amendments (passed by two-thirds of both the House and Senate) of which 27 have been ratified. Since 1978 Congress has only voted on 41 proposed amendments of the thousands introduced. Nine of those votes passed in the chamber in which it was introduced; the rest failed in the home chamber. Of the nine that passed in the home chamber, only one got a vote in the opposing chamber, the 1995 Balanced Budget Amendment. It passed the House 300 to 132 and failed in the Senate 65 to 35.

The 27 ratified amendments are below.

The first 10 are the bill of rights.

The 11th clarified the jurisdiction of the Supreme Court.

The 12th changed the way the president was elected.

The 13th, 14th, and 15th ended slavery and protected the rights of former slaves.

The 16th gave us income tax.

The 17th changed the way Senators are elected.

The 18th gave us prohibition.

The 19th gave women the right to vote.

The 20th changed the date the President takes office from March 4th to January 20th and the Congress to January 3rd and defines the succession of the presidency.

The 21st repealed prohibition.

The 22nd limits the President to two terms.

The 23rd grants the District of Columbia with electoral votes as though they were a state.

The 24th prohibits poll taxes.

The 25th provides for the event of a President's removal or incapacitation.

The 26th set the voting age to 18 years.

And the 27th, proposed in 1789 and ratified in 1992, provides that if Congress votes themselves a salary increase, there must be an intervening election before it is effective.

The 14th amendment had some controversy in its ratification. These controversies revolved around the states which had seceded from the union rejoining, and whether a state could first ratify the amendment and then reverse itself or reject the amendment and then reverse that.

Initially, Lincoln had presented a plan to congress to allow states to rejoin the union upon an oath of loyalty of 10 percent of its population, the 10% plan. Congress rejected this as too lenient, and passed the Wade-Davis Plan. They submitted it to Lincoln, who did not veto it, but then congress adjourned prior to the time period for a pocket veto. Having not been vetoed, and not returned to congress due to the adjournment, the bill failed. After Lincoln's assassination, President Johnson created a plan for re-entry which required that states: 1) abolish slavery, 2) repudiate the Confederate debt, 3) require a majority of voters to vow allegiance, and 4) ratify the 13th amendment. By June of

1866 10 of the 11 states had met these requirements; only Texas had not. However, since these states had written "black codes" into their laws, congress refused to seat the representatives until they were removed. This left an open question as to whether these states were part of the union.

On June 13, 1866, Congress proposed the 14th amendment. The Tennessee legislature ratified it on July 9th, 1866, and then was officially readmitted to the union on July 24th.

Question 1, can a state ratify an amendment prior to re-admission to the union? Does Tennessee's ratification count in the total of the numerator and the denominator of three-fourths? This did not seem to be an issue at the time but would come to the surface in June of 1867. The denominator would be the total number of states, 27 including Tennessee. On June 16th, 1867, Nebraska ratified the 14th amendment and became either the 20th or 21st state to do so. The three-fourths requirement would be 21, but does Tennessee count? Debate went on until January 15th 1868 when Illinois ratified, making 21 without Tennessee.

However, on the same day, Ohio rescinded their ratification, once again making the count 20 without Tennessee. This created question 2. Can a state ratify, and after the threshold of three-quarter has been met, rescind that ratification?

The debate was back on. Mercifully, Iowa ratified on March 9th, 1868. Then on March 24th New Jersey rescinded its ratification. Secretary of State Seward declared the amendment ratified after congress requested that he perform an analysis. No one knows who actually must declare an amendment ratified, but congress did eventually. The subject of counting will become even more convoluted when we look at state applications for an Article V convention.

What about the other six proposed amendments that were not ratified?

When Congress proposed the first set of amendments, there were twelve. The first two were not ratified with the Bill of Rights, but the second was ratified in 1992 becoming the 27th. The remaining one, referred to as the original first amendment, further defined the number of members of the House of Representatives, and should it be ratified would require about 7,000 members today instead of the 435 we have.

The unratified amendments are referred to as:
The Original First Amendment 1789 (or Apportionment Amendment)
Titles of Nobility 1810.
The Corwin Amendment 1861.
The Child Labor Amendment 1926.
The Equal Rights Amendment 1972.
The District of Columbia Voting Rights Amendment 1978.

Remember also that Article V calls for two methods of ratification, and Congress decides which one to use. Congress may choose State Legislatures or require State Conventions to determine ratification. Either way, three quarters of the States must ratify an amendment for it to become part of the Constitution. For the 27 amendments that have been ratified, and the six that have not, all have been directed to State Legislatures for ratification except one. The only one directed to State Conventions was the 21st, repeal of prohibition.

There is some controversy as to whether the Equal Rights Amendment was ratified or not. Congress proposed the amendment on March 22, 1972. Within the proposal, Congress set a ratification deadline of seven years, or March 22, 1979. Between 1972, and 1977, 35 States ratified the amendment. The requirement is three quarters of the several States, which would be 38. In 1978 Congress passed a resolution to extend the deadline to March 22, 1982. This is questionable on a couple of points. First, the original deadline had already expired. Second, the resolution to extend was only passed by a simple majority in both chambers but probably should have required two thirds. Eventually, a federal judge voided the extension. I question this on the basis that amending the Constitution is the exclusive domain of Congress and the States. In any event, no further States ratified the amendment prior to the 1982 deadline, so the questions are moot. However, three States, Nevada 2017, Illinois 2018, and Virginia 2020, have ratified it. Congress has made several attempts to extend the deadline again but has not had the votes. To further complicate the situation, six states have voted to rescind their ratification (no one knows if this is legitimate), four prior to the 1979 deadline, one prior to the 1982 deadline (if either the rescission or the deadline is valid) and one in 2021 (which begs all the above questions). The District of Columbia Voting Rights Amendment was very close on the vote. It passed the House on March 2, 1978 with 289 yes, 127 no, and 18 not voting. That's 434 votes. Rules of the House call for two-thirds to be calculated as the total votes (416) divided by 3 (138 & 2/3) times 2 (277 & 1/3) which rounds to 277 required for the two-thirds threshold. The 18 present-not-voting worked to the advantage of the yes vote by reducing the number of votes from 434 to 416, thus shrinking the two-thirds requirement from 289 to 277. The Senate vote was 67 yes, 32 no, and 1 not voting, close but a clear two-thirds by any count. The proposed amendment carried a seven-year sunset, meaning that it would expire on August 22, 1985 if three-quarters of the states (38) had not ratified it by that date. Only 16 states had done so by the expiration date. The effect of this amendment would have been that the District of Columbia would have had two Senators and a Representative as though they were a state. The twenty-third amendment provided for presidential electoral votes for the District of Columbia, and this amendment would have provided for that with the Congressional representation and repealed the twenty-third amendment. This was accomplished because the Democrats held a super-majority in the House and in the Senate, and this amendment would certainly have created two more Democrat Senators and another Democrat Representative. Would they have passed it if the DC population was more likely to result in increased Republican seats? Would a Republican supermajority have passed it had DC been more likely to increase Republican seats? May we conclude that this was about party politics more than it was about representation of the population of DC?

Yes, we may, and so it is good that the State Legislatures have a controlling role in the amendment process.

APPLICATIONS BY STATES FOR A CONVENTION

Since there have been nearly 12,000 attempts in Congress to propose amendments, only 33 of which were successful, and 27 ratified, what about the second method, a convention? Remember Article V related to the convention method reads as follows:

[Congress] on the Application of the Legislatures of two thirds of the several States, shall call a Convention for proposing Amendments....

Here are the statistics on States submitting applications to Congress to call a Convention for proposing amendments. There have been 450 applications filed with Congress from 1788 to 2023. About 82 are duplicates to a prior application by the same state for the same subject. 44 applications became moot when Congress proposed an amendment for that purpose, and it was ratified. 160 applications have been rescinded by the State making application. That leaves 164 valid and un-rescinded applications. Of the 50 States, only Hawaii has never filed an application with Congress. Of the 164 active applications, they belong to 40 different States.

Here is a list of the 40 States and the number of active applications for each:

Florida	11	Missouri	10
Alabama	9	Arkansas	10
Mississippi	9	Indiana	8
Illinois	7	Michigan	6
Nebraska	6	Wisconsin	6
California	5	Massachusetts	5
Pennsylvania	5	West Virginia	5
Iowa	4	Louisiana	4
North Dakota	4	Ohio	4
Alaska	3	Kentucky	3
North Carolina	3	Oregon	3
Rhode Island	3	Washington	3
Arizona	2	Connecticut	2
Georgia	2	Kansas	2
Minnesota	2	New York	2
Oklahoma	2	Tennessee	2
Texas	2	Utah	2
Vermont	2	Maine	1
New Hampshire	1	South Carolina	1
South Dakota	1	Wyoming	1

If two thirds of 50 States is 34, and 40 States have applications, why have we not called a convention? One of two reasons. The first possibility is that Congress is in dereliction of its mandatory duty to call a convention whenever 34 states have open applications. The second possibility is because all but four of the 164 open applications limit the subject matter of amendments to be proposed at a convention, and

Congress has decided that they need 34 with the same subject matter. No group of 34 States have indicated a common subject matter within their applications. In fact, there are 52 unique "subjects" identified to be considered in proposing amendments. The 52 counts as one of its subjects, no subject at all, which is the case of the 6 unlimited applications. When we consider just the active applications, there are only 42 subjects. Some of the 40 States have multiple active applications on file with different subjects. The most numerous States with open applications on the same subject are 26. So, the two thirds threshold is not currently met if the subject can be limited. The following chapters will discuss the subjects with the most active applications, and we will see if any subject has ever met the threshold of two-thirds of the states with active applications. As noted above, there are scholars who argue that the States may not limit the convention in any way, and consequently the subject is irrelevant. I have laid out the counts here as though the intent of the legislation to make an application for a specific subject means that they may be grouped, and that there can be duplicates, and that a congressionally proposed and ratified amendment might then make that application moot and no longer count as "active". Necessarily, the counts would be quite different if the subject is irrelevant, and may even void applications. Once again, the two key questions have not been finally answered, and that answer may only come with an actual convention, whether Congress calls it, or the States fill the void of Congress being in dereliction of its mandatory duty.

Below is a table showing the subjects and how many applications have been submitted for each one. The "All Other" line includes 29 subjects for which relatively few applications have ever been submitted. For each subject, the columns show how many are duplicates, how many were made moot by Congress proposing, and states ratifying an amendment, how many were rescinded by the submitting State, how many are active, the total number, and the years between the first submitted and the last submitted.

Subject Matter	Duplicate	Moot	Rescinded	Active	Total	Years
The Fist 105 Years 1788 - 1892	1	6	3	6	16	1788-1892
Direct election of Senators	32	28	-	-	60	1893-1911
Anti-polygamy	2	-	7	12	21	1906-1915
Repeal 16th	3	-	20	8	31	1939-1979
Revision of Article V	6	-	11	6	23	1939-2011
Balanced budget	15	-	21	26	62	1957-2017
Apportionment	10	-	20	13	43	1963-1969
Revenue sharing	2	-	8	9	19	1965-1972
Right to life	-	-	9	10	19	1973-1980
COS PROJ	-	-	2	19	21	2014-
The All-Other Group	11	10	59	55	135	1901-
Total	82	44	160	164	450	

In the following chapters we will review the history around most of these subjects. By that, I mean to say we will try to understand what the motivating factors were to prompt the States Legislatures to propose, debate, and pass resolutions which became the applications on file with Congress.

We will start by looking at the process which most State Legislatures follow in order to pass a resolution or any law for that matter. This is to provide some context within which to understand the difficulty of passing anything through a state legislature, let alone the same thing through 34 different legislatures.

Then a look at what a Convention of States is. You will see in the applications various descriptions of the "convention" which the state is asking for. The very first one, submitted by Virginia, calls for a "Convention of the States". Some call it an Article V Convention, others a Constitutional Convention, and perhaps there are other descriptors added to the word Convention. This is to say that some people get worked up with what the "convention for proposing amendments" should be called, but that concern is of no moment; the intent of the application is clear.

STATE LEGISLATURES & RESOLUTION PROCESS

Most State Legislatures are bicameral, meaning they have an Upper and Lower chamber. In fact, only Nebraska has a single chamber legislature. The numbers of members in each chamber and State varies dramatically. The highest number of members in the Lower chamber is 400 in New Hampshire, while the smallest is Alaska with 40. In the Upper chamber, the largest is 67 in Minnesota, and the smallest is 21 in Delaware and Nevada. In all 49 States, the total number in the Lower chamber is 5,413, an average of 111. The total in the Upper chamber in all 50 States is 1,973, an average of 40. This is important because these are the people which need to agree on a common resolution to call a Convention under Article V. If 34 States must agree on the same subject matter for which the Convention is being called, then they must pass that resolution with a simple majority in both chambers. In other words, there would have to be agreement by 1,904 people in the Lower chambers of 34 states and 714 in the Upper chambers of those same 34 States in order to call a Convention. That is roughly 2,618 in total, just to get a meeting to draft and debate proposed amendment language. Compare that to Congress who can pass a proposed amendment with 290 in the House and 67 in the Senate, a total of 357 people. The States have a much higher bar in order to propose any amendment.

The process in State legislatures is mostly the same. The first step is for a resolution to be drafted and sponsored by one member in either chamber. That Sponsor would file the bill in his home chamber. The bill would be referred to a committee.

The committee may decide not to hold a hearing, and the bill dies until next session. If the committee has a hearing, there would be public testimony and then vote. If the bill fails, it dies and starts over next session. If the vote is favorable, the bill would be sent to the floor of the full chamber.

The bill would be debated on the floor, and a vote taken. If the bill fails, it dies and starts over next session. If the vote is in favor of the bill, it would be sent to the opposing chamber for consideration.

The opposing chamber would go through the same committee process. If that committee failed the bill it would die until the next session, and the process would start from the beginning. If the bill passes committee, the full chamber would debate and vote. Should it fail on the floor, it would die until the next session, and the process would start from the beginning. If the bill passes on the floor, then it is submitted to Congress where it is read into the record of both the House and the Senate.

Now it's an application valid under Article V for Congress to call a Convention. This process must be repeated in 33 other State Legislatures in order to meet the criteria for Article V. This is further complicated if the 34 resolutions must indicate a common subject.

Clearly, this is a daunting process.

WHAT IS A CONVENTION OF STATES?

While the language in Article V refers to Congress calling a convention, it may not be obvious what this means to us today. From the point of view of the founding fathers in 1787, the meaning of a convention was well understood. From 1677 to 1774, the then Colonies had participated in at least 20 conventions. From 1776 to 2017, the now independent States have participated in at least an additional 22 conventions. Each of these are referred to as Conventions of States. A Convention of States is a temporary meeting of three or more States, attended by delegates authorized by the legislatures of each State, with instructions to debate about solutions to problems identified in the delegates instructions.

Early on, these conventions were used to plan a defense from, or plan a negotiation with, various Indian Tribes. By presenting a common face to a threat, they were able to present more power and have a better negotiating position. Starting with a convention in 1765 in response to the Stamp Act, the common threat became Great Britain, and finally in 1776 the Declaration of Independence was created and signed at a Convention of States. The Revolutionary War was managed, with a series of these Conventions and the Articles of Confederation were created and agreed to in the course of these.

After the Revolutionary War, the new independent States found themselves arguing over a range of trade issues and the Convention at Annapolis, MD, was called to try to resolve these. Only five States sent delegates, and the organizers sent out a notice to reconvene in Philadelphia in May 1787. While the convention in Philadelphia in 1787 became known as the Constitutional Convention, it was still a Convention of States.

Since the ratification of the Constitution, there have been many more Conventions of States, mostly regional to address specific issues for that region. The Northeastern States met in 1814 to discuss secession over the War of 1812. The Southern States met in 1850 and in 1861 in response to northern aggression and finally to write the Confederate Constitution.

Since the Civil War, there have been more Conventions of States. One was to propose antitrust measures and others. One resulted in the Lower and Upper Colorado River Compact in 1946-1949. The latest Convention of States was held in Phoenix, AZ, in 2017 to develop rules to be used in a potential convention to propose a Balanced Budget Amendment (more on this later).

The common threads in all 40 – 45 of these Conventions of States are important. They serve as precedent for any convention Congress might have to call in response to Article V Applications. Further, they serve as examples of what the creators of our Constitution meant by the word convention. One common thread is that the constituents are the States, each of which is represented by a delegation. Each State has one vote to be arrived at by that States delegation. The purpose and objective for each convention was clearly laid out in the call or invitation to send a delegation. The States have called, charged attending delegations, and upheld the results under their own sovereignty, not that of the United States. The federal or central government has had no role in any of these conventions, whether there was no central government, the central government was the Continental Congress under the Articles of Confederation, or the current federal government under our Constitution. So, when the founders agreed to the wording of Article V as, *[Congress] shall call a convention for proposing amendments*, they meant a Convention of States.

Looking at this another way, the States, under their own sovereignty, created a federal government using a Convention of States. They shared specific portions of their sovereignty with that federal government on specific subjects clearly identified in that Constitution. As a way to adjust the specific powers delegated to the federal government, the States may call another Convention of States to propose such amendments as defined in Article V thereof. To be sure, the States can call a Convention of States under their own sovereignty, outside of the parameters of the current Constitution to propose an entirely new form of government. However, if 34 States make application under Article V of this Constitution, and Congress performs its mandatory duty under this Constitution and calls a Convention of States based on the purpose articulated in those 34 applications, then that convention is bound to draft, debate, and propose amendments to this Constitution and not create and propose another.

All conventions have rules under which they do business. We may look to the conduct of any of the previous Conventions of States to understand the rules which governed their business. There are at least two recently created sets of rules which can also provide guidance.

The first set of rules were developed by Professor Rob Natelson, one of the leading Article V experts and Convention of States Project Co-Founder Michael Farris in 2015. These rules were then adopted for use in a mock Article V Convention of States hosted by the Convention of States Project in 2016. These rules are in Appendix 3.

Another set of rules was created and published by the most recent Convention of States held in Phoenix, Arizona, in 2017. This convention was attended by 19 States whose delegates were charged with proposing rules to govern a Convention of States which might be called to propose a Balanced Budget Amendment. These rules may be found in Appendix 4.

Perhaps the rules used in the Constitutional Convention from May to September of 1787 should also be considered. These may be found in Appendix 5. The last 6 of these rules were adopted on May 29th 1787. Five of these essentially held the member to secrecy as to the proceedings and debates. The debate on the secrecy had good points made on both sides. If daily reports were made publicly, delegates may be less inclined to change their minds on certain issues based on debates in the room. Also, knowing that their words might become public, delegates may be less inclined to propose innovative ideas for fear of public criticism. On the other hand, if the debates were open and discussed outside the hall, some better solutions may be missed from the lack of conversation and advice. Today, we all strive for transparency in our governments debates and processes and would most likely seek the same in any Convention of States to propose amendments.

For further reading on what a Convention of States is:
https://alec.org/article/a-convention-of-states-explained/
https://i2i.org/how-a-convention-of-states-really-works/
http://articlevinfocenter.com/wp-content/uploads/2021/03/QA.doc-final.pdf
https://civicsandcitizenship.org/what-is-convention-of-states/
https://www.frontline.news/post/convention-of-states-what-is-it-and-why-its-important

THE FIRST 105 YEARS 1788 - 1892

On September 17, 1787 the Philadelphia Convention completed its work on developing a new form of government as described in the new Constitution. Over the course of the previous four months some 55 men had taken part in the debates, some only in part, and on that day, there were 42 in the room. Being asked to sign their names to the document, three declined. George Mason from Virginia, Edmond Randolph Governor of Virginia and Elbridge Gerry of Massachusetts declined to sign because they felt the document should have specific prohibitions on the new government's ability to abridge the peoples' rights. They had been insistent on the inclusion of a Bill of Rights throughout the proceedings.

On September 18th the Pennsylvania Packet printed copies of the proposed Constitution, and on September 20th the Congress of the Confederation received their copies. On September 28th the Congress voted to send the proposed Constitution to the thirteen States for ratification by state conventions per Article VII. However, the day before, the first Anti-Federalist letter by Cato was published making an argument against the ratification of the Constitution. This was followed by letters from Centinel on October 5th, Federal Farmer on October 8th, and Brutus on October 18th all arguing against the new Constitution. Many more would follow, and today can be read together as the Anti-Federalist. On October 27th, the first of 85 articles was published in favor of the new Constitution. These can all be read together as The Federalist Papers. These were planned out in advance by Alexander Hamilton and James Madison; they and John Jay were to write them. Jay became ill, and the majority were written by the other two. Together, The Federalist Papers present the most accurate way to understand the meaning and intention of the Constitution, and The Anti-Federalist presents the contemporary argument against the Constitution.

Meanwhile, the States began to assemble conventions to debate and vote on the proposed Constitution. These conventions would meet, debate, and vote on accepting the Constitution over the next year.

Delaware convened their state convention on December 3rd 1787 and voted to ratify on December 7th, 1787, becoming the first State.

Pennsylvania was actually the first State to meet on November 20th, 1787, but with a high number of Anti-Federalists attending the convention, it took longer to get a ratification vote. The vote was 46 for and 23 against and was held on December 12th, 1787. The 23 members who voted against the Constitution got to work immediately to try and influence the other States to reject the new Constitution by sending a letter to them on December 18th, 1787. They included in the letter 14 proposed amendments which they believed would be needed for them to accept the Constitution. Here is the introductory paragraph to their 14 amendments which criticizes the process of debate and ratification more than it speaks of the 14 amendments they deemed necessary (Oswald, E, 1787). (The Address and reasons of dissent of the minority of the convention, of the state of Pennsylvania, to their constituents. https://www.loc.gov/resource/bdsdcc.c0401/)

The Convention met, and the same disposition was soon manifested in considering the proposed Constitution, that had been exhibited in every other stage of the business. We were prohibited by an express vote of the Convention, from taking any question on the separate articles of the plan, and reduced to the necessity of adopting or rejecting in toto. 'Tis true the majority permitted us to debate on each article, but restrained us from proposing amendments. They also determined not to permit us to enter on the minutes our reasons of dissent against any of the articles, nor even on the final question our reasons of dissent against the whole. Thus situated we entered on the examination of the proposed system of government, and found it to be such as we could not adopt, without, as we conceived, surrendering up your dearest rights. We offered our objections to the convention, and opposed those parts of the plan, which, in our opinion, would be injurious to you, in the best manner we were able; and closed our arguments by offering the following propositions to the convention.

Following this denunciation of the convention process and rules, the Pennsylvania Anti-Federalists listed their 14 suggested amendments. Most of the other States convention members voting no to the new Constitution would have seen their own State convention process in the same light.

New Jersey ratified unanimously, 38 – 0, on December 18th, 1787. Georgia on January 2nd, 1788 with a unanimous vote of 26 – 0.

Connecticut on January 9th with a vote of 128 – 40. None of these States proposed amendments with their letter of ratification.

Massachusetts ratified the Constitution on February 6th 1788, with a vote of 187 – 168. They then identified nine amendments in their letter notifying Congress of the ratification. The Pennsylvania Anti-Federalists had written a letter of dissent, suggesting amendments, to the other States, but Massachusetts included suggested amendments in their letter of transmittal to the Congress.

Rhode Island held a general referendum for March 24th, 1788, instead of a convention in keeping with Article VII. With a vote of 237 for and 2,708 against, the Constitution was soundly rejected.

Maryland ratified the Constitution on April 28, 1788, with a vote of 63 – 11 and did not include any suggested amendments in their letter. However, William Paca had proposed a list of about 20 amendments which were not accepted by the convention.

South Carolina became the eighth State to ratify with a vote of 149 – 73 on May 23rd, 1788. Their convention identified four items for which they suggested alteration.

New Hampshire had a convention from February 13 – 22, 1788, with no result. The convention reconvened on June 18th, and with a vote of 57 – 47 on June 21st became the ninth State to ratify. With that, the new Constitution became effective per the conditions laid out in Article VII. New Hampshire included 12 suggested amendments with their ratification letter.

Virginia became the 10th State when their convention ratified on June 25th, 1788, with a vote of 89 – 79. They included 20 suggested amendments in their ratification letter.

New York became the 11th State on July 26th, 1788, with a vote for ratification of 30 – 27. They identify 30 suggested amendments which they include in their ratification letter, and also in a circular letter to the other States. They go further by insisting that Congress make "an early and mature consideration" of all of the States suggested amendments.

On September 13th, 1788, with these 11 States, the Congress of the Confederation certified that the Constitution had been duly ratified, and set the date for the 1st Congress of the United States of America to meet on March 4th 1789.

So it was that with a backdrop of 11 States accepting the new Constitution and also asking for some 92 amendments, mostly repetitive, and the new Congress having yet to meet, the Virginia General Assembly passed a resolution to call a Convention of States for Proposing Amendments under Article V of the new Constitution. No other action could so define the lack of trust, existing in the new States, in the new Federal Government. A government, which in all actuality, did not yet exist.

Virginia was the first to attempt unleashing Article V. It was the heartfelt desire to protect individual liberty from an overpowerful federal government.

This will be the repetitive theme throughout the history of the States making applications to Congress under Article V. The Federal Government, in some action or perception, loses the trust of the State Legislatures, who then respond by making applications. To this day, the required number of States have not done so using the same subject matter to actually force Congress to call a convention, but then, that trust has not ever been completely restored either. I have included the resolution of the State of Virginia below:

(1 Annals of Cong. 258-59 (J. Gales, Sr. ed., 1834) (H.R., May 5, 1789))
In the General Assembly, November 14, 1788.

Resolved, That an application be made in the name and on behalf of the Legislature of this commonwealth to the Congress of the United States, in the words following, to wit: Convention

The good People of this Commonwealth, in Convention assembled, having ratified the Constitution submitted to their consideration, this Legislature has, in conformity to that act, and the resolutions of the United States in Congress assembled, to them transmitted, thought proper to make the arrangements that were necessary for carrying it into effect. Having thus shown themselves obedient to the voice of their constituents, all America will find that, so far as it depended on them, that plan of Government will be carried into immediate operation.

But the sense of the People of Virginia would be but in part complied with, and but little regarded, if we went no farther. In the very moment of adoption, and coequal with the ratification of the new plan of Government, the general voice of the Convention of this state pointed to objects no less interesting to the People we represent, and equally entitled to our attention. At the same time that, from motives of affection to our sister States, the Convention yielded their assent to the ratification, they gave the most unequivocal proofs, that they dreaded its operation under the present form.

In according to the Government under this impression, painful must have been the prospect, had they not derived consolation from a full expectation of its imperfections being speedily amended. In this resource, therefore, they placed their confidence, a confidence that will continue to support them whilst they have reason to believe that they have not calculated upon it in vain.

In making known to you the objections of the People of this Commonwealth to the new plan of Government, we deem it unnecessary to enter into a particular of its defects, which they consider as involving all the great and unalienable rights of freemen. For their sense on this subject, we beg leave to refer you to the proceedings of their late Convention, and the sense of the House of Delegates, as expressed in their resolutions of the thirtieth day of October, one thousand seven hundred and eighty-eight.

We think proper, however, to declare, that, in our opinion, as those objections were not founded in speculative theory, but deduced from principles which have been established by the melancholy example of other nations in different ages, so they will never be removed, and the cause itself shall cease to exist. The sooner therefore the public apprehensions are quieted, and the Government is possessed of the confidence of the People, the more salutary will be its operations, and the longer its duration.

The cause of amendments we consider as a common cause; and, since concessions have been made from political motives, which, we conceive, may endanger the Republic, we trust that a commendable zeal will be shown for obtaining those provisions, which, experience has taught us, are necessary to secure from danger the unalienable rights of human nature.

The anxiety with which our countrymen press for the accomplishment of this important end, will ill admit of delay. The slow forms of Congressional discussion and recommendation, if, indeed, they should ever agree to any change, would, we fear, be less certain of success. Happily for their wishes, the Constitution hath presented an alternative, by admitting the submission to a Convention of the States. To this, therefore, we resort as the source from whence they are to derive relief from their present apprehensions.

We do, therefore, in behalf of our constituents, in the most earnest and solemn manner, make this application to Congress, that a Convention be immediately called, of deputies from the several States, with full power to take into their consideration the defects of this Constitution that have been suggested by the State Conventions, and report such amendments thereto as they shall find best suited to promote our common interests, and secure to ourselves and our latest posterity, the great and unalienable rights of mankind.

JOHN JONES, Speaker Senate.

THOMAS MATHEWS, Speaker House Del.

During this time, from September 13th, 1788 through February 4th, 1789 the States held elections for President and Vice President as well as for Representatives to the House, and the various Legislatures were appointing Senators. George Washington was elected President and John Adams Vice President. Only ten States sent electors to the Electoral College on February 4th, 1789. Rhode Island and North Carolina had not yet ratified the Constitution and consequently could not vote. The New York Legislature failed to appoint its electors in time, and they were not represented. Perhaps that is due to the time spent working on their resolution to call a Convention of States under Article V.

That resolution is below *(H.R. Jour., 1st Cong., 1st Sess., 1789, p. 29-30)*:

State of New York,

In Assembly, February 5, 1789.

Resolved, If the honorable the Senate concur therein, that an application be made to the Congress of the United States of America, in the name and behalf of the Legislature of this State, in the words following, to wit: The People of the State of New York having ratified the Constitution agreed to on the seventeenth day of September, in the year of our Lord one thousand seven hundred and eighty-seven, by the Convention then assembled at Philadelphia, in the State of Pennsylvania, as explained by the said ratification, in the fullest confidence of obtaining a revision of the said Constitution by a General Convention; and in confidence rivet certain powers in and by the said Constitution granted, would not be exercised, until a Convention should have been called and convened for proposing amendments to the said Constitution: In compliance, therefore, with the unanimous sense of the Convention of this State, who all united in opinion that such a revision was necessary to recommend the said Constitution to the approbation and support of a numerous body of their constituents; and a majority of the members of which conceived several articles of the Constitution so exceptionable, that nothing but such confidence, and an invincible reluctance to separate from our sister States, could have prevailed upon a sufficient number to assent to it, without stipulating for previous amendments: And from a conviction that the apprehensions and discontents which those articles occasion, cannot be removed or allayed, unless an act to revise the said Constitution be among the first that Shall be passed by the new Congress: we, the Legislature of the State of New York, do, in behalf of our constituents, in the most earnest and solemn manner, make this application to the Congress, that a Convention of Deputies from the several States be called as early as possible, with full powers to take the said Constitution into their consideration, and to propose such amendments thereto, as they shall find best calculated to promote our common interests, and secure to ourselves and our latest posterity, the great and unalienable rights of mankind.

By order of the Assembly:

JOHN LANSING, Junior, Speaker.

In Senate, February 7, 1789.

By order of the Senate:

PIERRE VAN CORTLANDT, President. March 4, 1789 was the day the first U.S. Congress was to convene in New York City and begin the maiden task of standing up and forming an entirely new government. Moreover, because there was no quorum in the House or Senate, no business could be done at all. Eleven States had elected Representatives and appointed Senators and many were either in route to New York, or had not yet left home. Finally, on April 1st, the House of Representatives achieved a quorum and began doing business. On April 6th, the Senate achieved quorum and could begin business. They must create ways to collect revenues and pay bills, after all, they had assumed the revolutionary war debt from all of the States. Among all this turmoil, there were still 11 States, 8 of which had great expectations that the Congress would begin to propose some of the 92 amendments they had suggested.

Perhaps of all the 59 Representatives in the House, James Madison of Virginia was feeling the most pressure. After all, this structure of government was largely his suggestion in the Virginia plan. He needed it to work. It was a matter of Honor. More than that, he had made promises to his constituents back home that one of the first things would be to add a Bill of Rights. His colleagues were all busy creating the Tariff of 1789 to collect revenue, the Department of Foreign Affairs, the War Department, the Treasury Department, and the Judiciary Act to establish the federal courts. All of these were being proposed, debated, adjusted, and debated some more. And in the middle of all this, on June 8th, 1789, James Madison rose and asked that they form a Committee of the Whole to review and debate 17 proposed amendments.

Madison realized what most of his fellow representatives did not. He had been one of the most vocal opponents of adding a Bill of Rights. But now, he could see that if the Congress did not propose these amendments according to Article V, the States would soon have the 9 required applications to call a Convention of States and propose their own amendments. He also saw what his fellow Representatives did see, that there was no experience with how this government would work, and they were very reticent to make any changes before they knew what did not work. Madison finally hounded the House enough to prevail, and they passed the bill of 17 amendments on August 24th, and sent them to the Senate. The Senate made alterations and consolidations, and on September 9th passed a slate of 12 amendments. On September 25th, the House and Senate agreed on the 12 amendments and sent them to the States for approval.

The approval would require three quarters of the State Legislatures to ratify them and add them to the Constitution. Three quarters of 11 is 8.25, so 9 States would be required. North Carolina ratified the Constitution on November 21, 1789, and Rhode Island finally joined on May 29, 1790. This moved the threshold to 10 States required for ratification of the Bill of Rights. On December 15th, 1791, 10 of the 12 amendments reached that threshold and became what we know as the Bill of Rights. The first and second of the original 12 remained unratified. The second was finally ratified in 1992 and became the 27th amendment.

The first one, now referred to as "The Original First Amendment", would set the number of Representatives in the House to not less than 1 for every 50,000 in population, and the seats would be apportioned to the States based on the population. This would have made our House of Representatives today have about 7,000 members. Instead, we have 435 as a result of the Apportionment Act of 1929. In 1929, 435 was about one Representative for every 230,000 in population, today that is about one for every 805,000.

If the Founding Fathers thought that "representation" was adequate at one for each 50,000 people, would they find for every 805,000 unacceptable? Would the members of Congress who crafted and passed the Apportionment Act of 1929, seeing one for 230,000 as adequate, find one for 805,000 adequate? Never mind what the Founding Fathers or the 1929 Congress thought might be appropriate representation. Do you think you can be adequately represented being one of 805,000?

If not, perhaps it is time to unleash Article V and insist on a number at which each of us may feel represented. If not one in 805,000 or 230,000 or 50,000, let's find that number. The question of what your future holds depends on your participation. Your participation with your state legislator will help generate the political will to unleash Article V.

At any rate, by the end of 1791, the Constitution now contained a full Bill of Rights, capsulated in the first 10 amendments. But for now, there were only two Article V applications in the congressional record, and they had been made moot by the proposal and ratification of the first 10 amendments. The States and the Congress seemed to be content with the operations of the Federal Government for the next 40 years. Although Congress had proposed and the States had ratified the 11th and 12th amendments, there was very little division of the country over the Constitution.

The Federal Government enacted the Tariff of 1828, which placed import duties on foreign goods to protect the U.S. manufacture of similar goods. The result was a reduced revenue for foreign manufacturers which caused those countries to place a tariff on U.S. exports. The combination of these two events was to improve the economies of the industrial northern states, and devastate the economies of the agricultural southern states. The southern states called these the Tariff of Abominations and argued that the Federal Government had no authority to pass such an uneven law. They began to take up the assertion that the States had the right to 'Nullify' federal laws that they deemed unconstitutional. These arguments resulted in the Legislatures of Georgia and South Carolina to make Article V applications for the purpose of making an amendment to Clarify the 10th Amendment. Then in 1833, Alabama made an Article V application for the purpose of making a Tariff Amendment. In the end, further negotiations in Congress prompted compromises which reduced tensions. Once again, Constitutional Amendment conversations quieted for nearly 30 years.

In the late 1850s, with the tensions over the expansion of slavery increased, the southern States once again felt the overreach of the Federal Government. The northern States, likewise agitated by abolitionists, wanted very much to curtail the expansion of slavery while preserving the Union.

On December 20, 1860, South Carolina seceded from the union. Four days later they published their Declaration of Secession which indicted the northern States with violations of Article IV, of the Constitution since 1852. They went on to say that the federal government had become complicit in those violations through non-enforcement of the Constitution. Between January 25th and March 14th of 1861, Kentucky, New Jersey, Indiana, and Illinois made an application for an Article V Convention so that a solution may be found to save the union. The words are so poignant that they require inclusion here:

(Cong. Globe, 36th Cong., 2d Sess. 751, S., Feb. 5, 1861) Kentucky 1/25/1861 –
Whereas the people of some States feel themselves deeply aggrieved by the policy and measures which have been adopted by the people of some other States; and whereas an amendment of the Constitution of the United States is deemed indispensably necessary to secure them against similar grievances in the future: therefore--
Resolved,... That application to Congress to call a convention for proposing amendments to the Constitution of the United States, pursuant to the fifth article, thereof, be, and the same is hereby, now made by this general assembly of Kentucky; and we hereby invite our sister States to unite with us without delay, in similar applications to Congress.

(Cong. Globe, 36th Cong., 2d Sess. 680, S., Feb. 1,1861) New Jersey 2/1/1861 –
Whereas the people of New Jersey, conforming to the opinion of "the Father of his Country," consider the unity or the Government, which constitutes the people of the United States one people, the main pillar in the edifice of their Independence, the support of their tranquility at home and peace abroad, of their prosperity, and of that liberty which they so highly prize; and properly estimating the immense value of their national Union to their Individual happiness, they cherish a cordial, habitual, and immovable attachment to it as the palladium of their political safety and prosperity: Therefore

- *Be it resolved by the Senate and General Assembly of the State of New Jersey, That It Is the duty of every good citizen, in all suitable and proper ways, to stand by and sustain the Union of the States as transmitted to us by our fathers.*

- *And be it resolved, That the Government of the United States is a National Government, and the Union it was designed to perfect is not a mere compact or league; and that the Constitution was adopted in a spirit of mutual compromise and concession by the people of the United States, and can only be preserved by the constant recognition of that spirit.*
- *And be it resolved, that however undoubted may be the right of the General Government to maintain its authority and enforce its laws over all parts of the country, it is equally certain that forbearance and compromise are indispensable at this crisis to the perpetuity of the Union; and that it is the dictate of reason, wisdom, and patriotism, peacefully to adjust whatever differences exist between the different sections of our country.*
- *And be it resolved, That the resolutions and propositions submitted to the Senate of the United States by JOHN J. CRITTENDEN, of Kentucky, for the compromise of the questions in dispute between the people of the northern and of the southern States, or any other constitutional method of settling the slave question permanently, will be acceptable to the people of the State of New Jersey, and the Senators and Representatives in Congress from New Jersey be requested, and earnestly urged, to support these resolutions and propositions.*
- *And be it resolved, that as the Union of these States is in imminent danger unless the remedies before suggested be speedily adopted, then, as a last resort, the State of New Jersey hereby makes application, according to the terms of the Constitution, of the Congress of the United States, to call a convention (of the States) to propose amendments to said Constitution.*
- *And be it resolved, That such of the States as have In force laws which interfere with the constitutional rights of citizens of the other States either regard to their persons or property, or which militate against the just construction of that part of the Constitution that provides that the" citizens of each State shall be entitled to all the privileges and immunities of citizens in the several States, are earnestly urged and requested, for the sake of peace and the Union, to repeal all such laws.*
- *And be it resolved, that his Excellency, Charles S. Olden, Peter D. Vroom Robert F. Stockton, Benjamin Williamson, Joseph F.*

Randolph; Frederick T. Frelinghuysen, Rodman M. Price, Thomas J. Stryker, and William C. Alexander be appointed commissioners to confer with Congress, and our sister States, and urge upon them the importance of carrying into effect the principles and objects of the foregoing resolutions.

- And be it resolved, That the commissioners above named, in addition to their other powers, be authorized to meet with those now or hereafter to be appointed by our sister State of Virginia, and such commissioners of other States as have been or may here-after be appointed, to meet at Washington on the 4th day of February next.

- And be it resolved, that copies of the foregoing resolutions be sent to the President of the Senate and Speaker of the House of Representatives of the United States, and to the Senators and Representatives in Congress from New Jersey, and to the Governors of the several States.

(Cong. Globe, 37th Cong., Special Sess. 1465-66, S., Mar. 18, 1861)
Indiana 3/11/1861 –

A joint resolution requesting Congress to call a convention to amend the Constitution of the United States.

Be it resolved by the General Assembly of the State of Indiana, That while we regard the Constitution of the United States, if properly interpreted and duly enforced, as amply sufficient to secure the just rights of the people of all the States of the Union, still as dissatisfaction and misunderstandings have arisen respecting the proper interpretation of that instrument, the Congress of the United States is hereby requested to call a convention of the several States, in accordance with the fifth article of the Constitution thereof, to take into consideration the propriety of amending the same, so that its meaning may be definitely understood In all sections of the Union.

(1861 Ill. Laws 281-82) Illinois 3/14/1861 –

WHEREAS, although the people of the State of Illinois do not desire any change in our Federal constitution, yet as several of our sister States have indicated that they deem it necessary that some amendment should be made thereto; and whereas, in and by the fifth article of the *constitution of the United States, provision is made for proposing amendments to that instrument, either by congress or by a convention ; and whereas a desire has been expressed, in various parts of the United States, for a convention to propose amendments to the constitution ; therefore,*

Be it resolved by the General Assembly of the State of Illinois, that if application shall be made to Congress, by any of the States deeming themselves aggrieved, to call a convention, in accordance with the constitutional provision aforesaid, to propose amendments to the constitution of the United States, that the Legislature of the State of Illinois will and does hereby concur in making such application.

Resolved, That, until the people of these United States shall otherwise direct, the present Federal Union must be preserved as it is, and the present constitution and laws must be administered as they are; and, to this end, in conformity with that constitution and the laws, the whole resources of the State of Illinois are hereby pledged to the Federal authorities.

Resolved, that copies of the above preamble and resolutions be sent to each of our Representatives and Senators in Congress and to the executives of the several States.

Can you hear the desperation in these written words? The very Union was at stake, and these legislatures were pulling out all the stops to work just one more compromise. Just one more try at a peaceful solution. It is too bad that this issue was over the treatment of humans considered property. If only the issue had been purely property, for example, guns or gas-powered vehicles. Perhaps even people of another type, like the unborn. Would we have been able to compromise if we had a convention instead of a war?

These states were trying to exercise the power of Article V to accomplish what Congress could not. Were there a Convention of States with delegates assigned by state legislatures, would they have achieved a resolution which Congress could not? Could that resolution have taken the form of an amendment which three-quarters of the states could have ratified? This is the promise of the power of unleashing Article V.

Congressman Thomas Corwin of Ohio proposed an amendment to protect slavery from federal interference. It was sent to the States for ratification in March 1861. The Corwin amendment was never ratified. Nothing came of the five Article V applications either, and in 1864, Oregon filed an Article V application, recognizing that slavery was the main cause of the Civil War, to propose amendments to end it. All of these were made moot by the ultimate proposal and ratification of the 13th, 14th, and 15th Amendments.

Once again, suggestions to amend the Constitution went away for about 30 years. From 1788 to 1892 the Congress had proposed a total 18 amendments of which 15 had been ratified. The States had submitted a mere 16 Article V Applications without ever reaching the two thirds threshold. These facts may lead to two conclusions. First, that the Constitution had proven to have few if any flaws, and they had been mitigated by compromise or amendment. Second, that the Federal Government, with a few exceptions, was operating within the confines of the Constitution. We will see that neither of these conclusions can be claimed about the next 130 years. It seems that the words of James Madison in Federalist 85, "We may safely rely on the disposition of the State legislatures to erect barriers against the encroachments of the national authority" were largely accurate.

In the 20th and 21st centuries, it seems every day that the Federal Government is finding ways to limit some of those rights, ways to find new rights as though the government grants them, or just ignoring the concept of individual rights altogether. Is it time to reassert our self-governing authority as We the People, or at least for the States to reassert their retained sovereignty by calling for a Convention of States under Article V to clarify the meaning of the words in the Constitution? The Supreme Court has spent 200 years defining those words by stretching some and compressing others to get an outcome they like. At least 434 more times, a State has decided that they need to unleash the power of Article V.

In the next 11 sections, I will endeavor to tell the stories of how the states came to submit an additional 434 applications in their efforts, mostly, to erect a barrier between the people and the federal government. We will cover them in the following sections:

The graph below depicts the number of applications filed, the number of applications rescinded and the number of active applications since 1900. Notations identify the nine subjects of the bulk of filed applications, and the rescissions based on congress proposed amendments being ratified and the points where some states rescinded all applications.

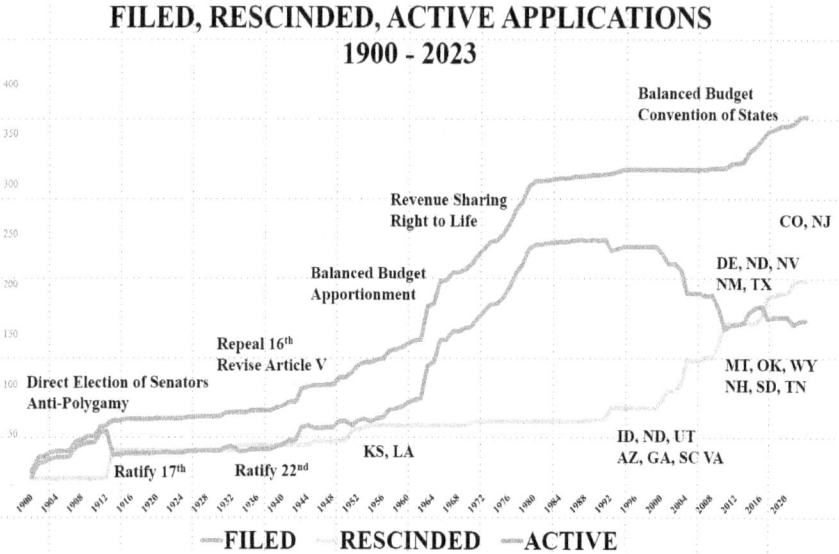

FILED, RESCINDED, ACTIVE APPLICATIONS
1900 - 2023

DIRECT ELECTION OF SENATORS

The Constitution in Article I, Section 3, clauses 1 and 2 says that Senators will be elected by State Legislatures. Each State has two Senators, each with one vote in the U.S. Senate. This was a result of the Large vs. Small State compromise in the Constitutional Convention. However, the election by Legislatures was supported by all in attendance, save James Wilson of Pennsylvania, who favored popular election of Senators. The election by State Legislatures was designed to provide for the States to have representation in the Federal Government, and protect States from losing more power than the Constitution had granted. Senators were divided into three classes with one third of the total in each class. Every two years, one class of Senators would be up for reelection.

Interestingly, while there was only one opponent at the Constitutional Convention to State Legislatures electing Senators, the public debates as well as the debates in the House of Representatives continued. In 1826 there was an amendment proposed to the House for the popular election of Senators. In 1829 and in 1855 similar bills were proposed. None of these passed. In 1868, President Andrew Johnson proposed the idea as well. Of course, the opposing views were also still present in Congress. With the two-party system firmly established by the 1830s and 1840s, the parties in State Legislatures would caucus and work out who their senatorial candidate would be. Normally, the party with the majority would then name their candidate the Senator. Factions in the majority party would sometimes create an opportunity for the minority party to elect the Senator. In some cases, two candidates would seek popular support hoping to influence the votes of legislators. Perhaps the most famous example of this would be the Lincoln vs. Douglas contest in Illinois in 1858. As time went on, many argued that the elections by State Legislatures would, and did create corruption in those seeking seats in the U.S. Senate. For example, many Senators acted as "bosses" in State party politics thus ensuring their own reelections. Roscoe Conkling would be a good example of this with his running the party from the New York Customs House.

Throughout the 1860s the debate went on. The House and Senate voted to veto the appointment of John P. Stockton of New Jersey because he was elected by a plurality instead of a majority. In 1866, Congress passed legislation that required Senators be elected by an absolute majority. While this new law gave consistency to the State process of electing Senators, it did not end the electoral deadlocks. Governors could still appoint Senators to fill vacancies provided that the State Legislature was not in session. However, in 1893 the Senate refused to seat Senators so appointed. The situation in Delaware was so bad, they did not elect a Senator for four years. From 1891 to 1905, State Legislatures deadlocked 46 times and consequently failed to elect Senators 14 times.

Corruption remained a concern; however, fewer than 10 cases were contested on the basis of impropriety between 1866 and 1906. In the end, only one election was voided. In 1900 it was determined that William A. Clark of Montana had bribed members of the State Legislature to win his 1899 bid for a Senate seat, and the U.S. Senate refused to seat him. He ran again and served as Montana Senator from 1901 to 1907. The fact that there were no other hard facts to support the corruption claims in general, the perception that State Legislatures electing Senators was a corrupt business persisted.

Another very real problem was the time consumed by State Legislatures in the selection of Senators. Two out of every six years State Legislatures were so involved in the question of Senators that in many States this resulted in the Legislatures ignoring other needed legislation. In many cases, this produced a deadlock in the Legislature, and no Senator was elected. This would most often occur in States where the two chambers of their legislature were controlled by opposing parties. Consequently, the State went without representation in the Senate due to the vacancy. Many States election processes required that the two chambers would meet in a joint session to resolve an impasse. Even this did not work effectively when in 1855, Democrats in Indiana, California and Missouri refused to attend the joint session thus denying quorum and leaving their Senate seats vacant until 1857.

Amendments for Direct Election of Senators had been introduced at least 287 times in Congress. The Populist Party made Direct Election of Senators a plank in their platform in the mid-1890s. The amendment was introduced in the House of Representatives every year from 1893 to 1902. Nebraska was the State with the most foresight, submitting a resolution in 1893 for an Article V Convention to propose an amendment for direct election of senators. Oregon was the first State to solve the problem with a law that their national elections ballot every two years would include a "referendum" vote for Senators, and State Legislators were required to vote for the candidate who won the primary referendum. This became known as the "Oregon Plan", and many States enacted similar laws.

The Oregon Plan did not fix the problem nation-wide, so it was that in 1901, the following states in quick succession filed applications for a Convention; Nebraska 4/14/1893, Pennsylvania 2/13/1901, Idaho 2/21/1901, Montana 2/21/1901, Oregon 2/23/1901, Missouri 3/12/1901, North Carolina 3/13/1901, Tennessee 3/20/1901, Colorado 4/1/1901, Texas 4/17/1901, Arkansas 4/21/1901, and Michigan 5/8/1901. All of the applications contained very similar versions of the language which Kentucky used (*45 Cong. Rec. 7115, 1910*):

Resolution favoring a change In the Constitution of the United States so as to provide for the-election of Senators in the Congress of the United States by popular vote.

Whereas a large number of state legislatures have at various times adopted memorials and resolutions in favor of election of United States Senators by popular vote; and

Whereas the National House of Representatives has on four separate occasions within recent years adopted resolutions in favor of this proposed change in the method of electing United States Senators, which was not adopted by the Senate; and

Whereas by reason of alleged corruption and fraud and the corrupt use of money, the election of United States Senators in several States has been prevented and by deadlocks several States have failed to elect Senators and in a number of instances the will of the people prevented; and

Whereas Article V of the Constitution of the United States provides that Congress, on the application of two-thirds of the several States, shall call a convention for proposing amendments, and believing there is a general desire upon the part of the people of Kentucky that United States Senators should be elected by the people,

Be it resolved by the general assembly of the Commonwealth of Kentucky, That the legislature of the State of Kentucky favors the adoption of an amendment to the Constitution which shall provide for the election of the United States Senators by popular vote, and joins with other States of the Union in respectfully requesting that a convention be called for the purpose of proposing an amendment to the Constitution of the United States, as provided for in Article V of the said Constitution, which amendment shall provide for a change in the present method of electing United States Senators, so that they can be chosen in each State by a direct vote of the people.

Resolved, that a copy of this concurrent resolution and application to Congress for the calling of a convention be sent to the President of the United States Senate and the Speaker of the House of Representatives.

Between 1902 and 1911 an additional 15 States submitted their applications for an Article V Convention to propose an amendment for the direct election of senators. This brought the total number of applications in the congressional record for this purpose to 28. The 2/3 requirement for congress to call a convention would have been 32 states.

According to Andrew Glass (2016), one of the first Socialist members of the House of Representatives, Victor Berger of Wisconsin, proposed an amendment on April 27, 1911. He opened his proposal with:

Whereas the Senate in particular has become an obstructive and useless body, a menace to the liberties of the people, and an obstacle to social growth; a body, many of the Members of which are representatives neither of a State nor of its people, but solely of certain predatory combinations, and a body which, by reason of the corruption often attending the election of its Members, has furnished the gravest public scandals in the history of the nation....

Berger's amendment would have eliminated the Senate and removed the President's veto over the House of Representatives law making power, and the courts judicial review as well. Of course, the socialist view was that the people's representatives should be the only authority in making laws. Berger was not well liked in the House, and left in 1913. He was convicted under the Espionage Act and sentenced to 20 years in prison for speaking against the U.S. participation in World War One. His sentence was invalidated in 1921. In 1918 he lost a three-way Senate race. Late that year he won reelection to the House, but they refused to seat him. Once his conviction was overturned in 1921, he was reelected and served from 1923 to 1929. His amendment quietly died in committee.

Perhaps Berger's radical proposed solution had an impact on the Senate. Also, many States had adopted the Oregon Plan, and many Senators had now been elected accordingly. Senators could also see that if Congress did not propose an amendment an Article V Convention was inevitable. So, in 1912, when the House once again passed the proposed 17th amendment, the Senate had the votes and followed suit. Having passed both houses with 2/3, Congress sent the proposed amendment to the states. The 17th amendment was ratified by ¾ of the states in 1913.

While this finally seemed to fix the problem of vacancies and the perception of corruption in the Senate, there remains an open question as to whether States are fairly represented. Remember that a key aspect of the State Legislatures appointing Senators was to ensure that the State had representation in the federal government. By popular vote, now the people are represented in the House and in the Senate. In 2023 the Senate had 49 Republicans while 29 State Legislatures were majority Republican. There are 48 Democrats in the Senate and 3 Independents who lean Democrat, but only 20 State Legislatures are majority Democrat. Virginia's Legislature is split, with a Republican majority in the lower House of Delegates, and a Democrat majority in the upper Senate. If Senators appointed by Legislatures assumed the party of their States Legislatures, the Senate would be 57 Republicans, and 43 Democrats. One could make a serious argument that the States, nor the people are fairly represented in the Senate. There must be a better answer to restore the role of the Senate. We will see in the Apportionment section this issue raised in a slightly different way. Every

State has a set of needs and situations which will vary dramatically from those of the majority of its population. These needs require representation just as much as people do, and that is what has been lost with the direct election of Senators.

So, between the one of 805,000 representation in the House, and the direct election of Senators, can there truly be a constituency of people which guide these people in Congress? By design of the Constitution, the House was to represent the people and the Senate was to represent the states. The Apportionment Act of 1929, combined with 17th amendment has eroded representation of either constituency intended, and left open a greater ability for personal preference and special interests to override the desires of the people or the states. This is clearly a reason for both the people, through their state legislators and the state legislatures as a whole, to unleash the power of Article V.

Below is a graph showing the number of states with new applications, rescissions and active applications by year:

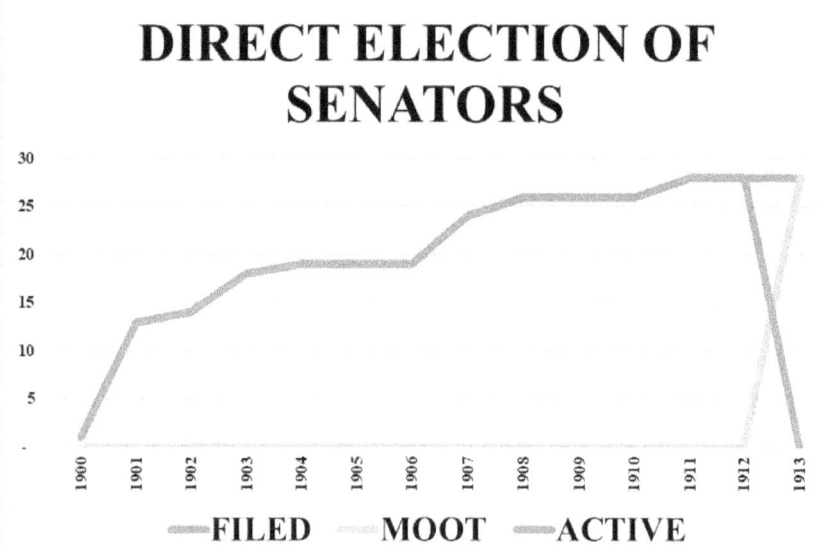

ANTI-POLYGAMY AMENDMENT

Throughout history, the structure and relationships of the core family has taken many forms. Without doubt, one-man, one-woman has been the dominant structure of most societies. Rulers and the aristocracy have often adopted a one-man, many-women structure, even while the bulk of the people in their societies have retained the one-man, one-woman family structure.

A recent study of 130 countries by Pew Research, looked at polygamy around the world and found that about 2% of the global population lives in polygamous households. However, in the vast majority of countries, that percentage is less than 0.5%. Polygamy is over 10% in sub-Saharan African countries. Many of the countries that permit polygamy are Muslim majority, but fewer than 1% of Muslim men have more than one wife. While the Jewish Torah and Christian Old Testament contain examples of polygamy, both religions disavowed the practice in the Middle Ages. Polyandry, one-woman many-men structures are even more rare, to the point most people are not familiar with the term.

So, what about America? To say the least, our puritan beginnings would have frowned on the concept. Over the 150 or so years from then to the creation of our Constitution, not much had changed in the American view of any relationship between a man and woman outside of a one-man, one-woman marriage.

But then, enter Joseph Smith, founder of the Church of Latter-day Saints, and his receiving Section 132 in 1830, and in keeping with that revelation took his first plural wife in 1835. From then until 1852, polygamy still was not openly practiced in the Mormon church. In 1852, Orson Pratt, an apostle, made a public speech defending polygamy as a tenet of the Mormon Church. From then until 1890, Mormon church leaders preached and encouraged the practice of multiple wives. Nonetheless, the majority of Mormons did not practice polygamy. Instances varied from as little as 5% in some communities to as much as 40% in others.

The reaction of the rest of the country to the polygamous practices of the Mormons was negative and harsh. The Republican Party in 1854 declared polygamy and slavery the "twin relics of barbarism". Congress passed the Morrill Act in 1862 prohibiting plural marriage in the territories, and it disincorporated the Mormon church. Because the country was in the middle of the Civil War, the law was not enforced. In 1867, the Utah Territorial Legislature asked that the Morrill Act be repealed. Congress responded with the Cullom Bill to strengthen the Morrill Act. While it did not pass as a whole bill, most of it became law in pieces over time. Many other anti-polygamy bills were introduced in the early 1870s. Most did not pass until 1874 when the Poland Act became law.

For their part, the Mormons continued with the practice of plural marriage believing that freedom of religion in the first amendment protected it. In keeping with that belief, George Reynolds agreed to go to trial under the anti-polygamy laws. His case reached the Supreme Court in 1879 (*Reynolds v. United States, 1879*). The court held that:
Laws are made for the government of actions, and while they cannot interfere with mere religious belief and opinion, they may with practices.

It seems that we can believe whatever we want, we can preach whatever we want, but it may not be legal to practice what we preach.

Isn't this the crux of law making in a free society? We may believe whatever we want, and we may speak of what we believe, but our actions become the governable item. We agree that a government of a free society is intended to protect the life, liberty, and property of its citizens. We then also agree that limiting actions by law is how that protection is accomplished. However, the First Amendment of the U.S Constitution reads:
Congress shall make no law respecting an establishment of religion, or prohibiting the free exercise thereof...".

Isn't action the very essence of exercising a religious belief? This is not to say that all actions claimed to be based on religious beliefs should be automatically acceptable. Shouldn't the first question be "How does this action injure the life, liberty, or property of another?". Provided that the participants in plural marriages are all adults and have consented to the arrangements, who then is the injured party?

Nonetheless, in 1882 Congress passed the Edmunds Act, which amended the Morrill Act. Polygamy was now a felony and had a punishment of up to five years imprisonment and a $500 fine. Even unlawful cohabitation, which did not require the proof of a marriage ceremony, was punishable by six months in jail and a $300 fine. Because it was a felony, convictions also removed the right to vote or hold office. This resulted in the dismissal of all election officers in Utah Territory, and five commissioners were appointed to direct elections.

This still did not control polygamy in Utah, and in 1887 Congress passed the Edmunds-Tucker Bill. This required plural wives to testify against their husbands. It also dissolved the Perpetual Emigrating Fund Company which helped Mormon church members move to Utah. Beyond that, it provided a mechanism for the government to acquire the property of the church.

With all this pressure two things began to happen in the Mormon church. Those members practicing polygamy went into hiding to avoid arrest or having to testify in trials. Leaders, however, could not hide, and finally on September 26th, 1890, Wilford Woodruff, church President, issued a press release called the Manifesto, advising the Latter-day Saints to refrain from plural marriages. The church's general conference approved that measure on October 6, 1890, and polygamy was officially ended in the Mormon church. This sounds like an end to the problem. Far from it. Not all members stopped entering plural marriages, and new ones continued to be formed. Nothing was said about how to handle existing plural marriages. In fact, all of the general authorities of the church which were members of polygamous marriages continued to cohabit with all of their plural wives. Further, most of the members in plural arrangements followed the example of leadership and things stayed just as they were. To complicate things further, Mormons in Mexico openly practiced polygamy, and Canada only stipulated that Mormon men could have only one wife in Canada. Many had a wife in Canada and another in America.

Utah Territory became a State in 1896. In 1903, the Utah State Legislature appointed Reed Smoot to a Senate Seat. Reed Smoot was a monogamist, but a member of the Mormon church and a member of the Quorum of the Twelve Apostles. Instead of seating him in 1904, the Senate started a series of hearings to decide whether to seat him or expel him. These hearings went on until 1907 when a vote fell short of the two-thirds required to expel him. However, the hearings shed light on the fact that polygamy was alive and well in Utah and the Mormon church. The hearings prompted the Mormon Church President, Joseph F. Smith to issue what is called the "Second Manifesto" on April 7, 1904. This time, the Manifesto had teeth. It provided for the end to all plural marriages with excommunication for those who refused to end their plural marriages. By 1910, the church had adopted a new policy based on the new Manifesto. Communities of Fundamentalists who believed that the church gave in to government pressure continued the practice of polygamy and have been excommunicated.

The Senate investigation not only showed a light for the LDS leadership to see, but for the entire nation to realize that anti-polygamy laws had not been enforced and had not ended the practice in America. New York was the first State to send its application to Congress for an Article V Convention to propose an Anti-Polygamy amendment reading (*40 Cong. Rec. 4551, 1906*):

STATE OF NEW YORK

In Senate, Albany, March 1, 1906.

Whereas, it appears from the investigation recently made by the Senate of the United States, and otherwise, that polygamy still exists in certain places in the United States notwithstanding prohibitory statutes enacted by the several States thereof, and

Whereas the practice of polygamy is generally condemned by the people of the United States and there is a demand for the more effectual prohibition thereof by placing the subject under Federal Jurisdiction and control, at the same time reserving to each State the right to make and enforce its own laws relating to marriage and divorce; now, therefore,

Resolved (if the assembly concur), That application be and hereby is made to Congress, under the provisions of article 5 of the Constitution of the United States for the calling of a convention to propose an amendment to the Constitution of the United States whereby polygamy and polygamous cohabitation shall be prohibited and Congress shall be given power to force such prohibition by appropriate legislation.

Resolved, That the legislatures of all other States of the United States, now in session or when next convened, be and they are hereby respectfully requested to Join in this application by the adoption of this or an equivalent resolution.

Resolved further, That the secretary of state be and he hereby is directed to transmit copies of this application to the Senate and House of Representatives of the United States, and to the several Members of said body representing this State therein; also, to transmit copies hereof to the legislatures of all other States of the United States.

Three more States, Delaware, West Virginia and Pennsylvania filed their applications in 1907 with virtually the same language. Washington, South Dakota, and Minnesota presented their resolutions in 1909. In 1911, Nebraska, Ohio, Tennessee, Montana, Oklahoma, and Texas added their States to the list. Vermont joined in 1912, and in 1913, Illinois, Michigan, Wisconsin, and Oregon made their applications. South Carolina was the late comer in 1915 bringing the total number of states to 19 falling short of the required two-thirds or 32 states. All of these applications remained open and active until 2004 when some states began to clean up their list of applications. So far, seven have been rescinded leaving 11 open and active applications.

The next page contains a graph showing the number of states with new applications, rescissions, and active applications by year:

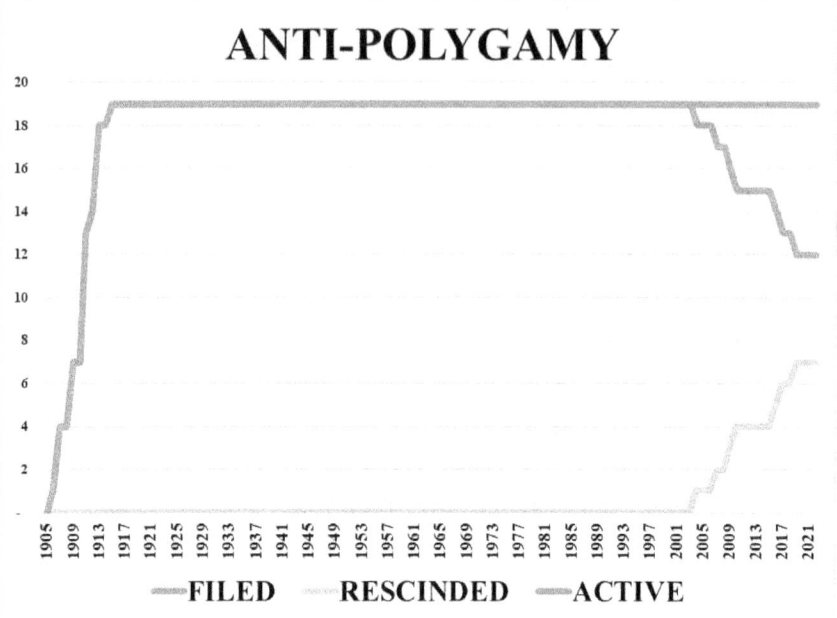

REPEAL THE 16TH AMENDMENT

From the earliest days of European settlement of North America through the 1850s, the economic model of the South became more and more centered first on slave labor, and second on cotton. In conflict with the increase in slavery, was the growing concept of individual rights, freedoms and the equality of all men. No one better promoted this idea than the minister of the Congregational church in Chebacco Parish in Ipswich, Massachusetts. John Wise (1652-1725) was an early and loud opponent to the overreach of the British government. His sermons and books were the lessons of liberty that would be the model for the revolutionaries three generations later. His sermons reprinted in 1772 used biblical references to support the following concepts:

1. God created all men equal and every man must be acknowledged equally by the state.
2. The end of all good government is to protect every man's life, liberty, estate, and honor.
3. Legitimate government only exists with the consent of the governed.
4. Taxation without representation is tyranny.

These concepts all show up in the Declaration of Independence, but more importantly, fly in the face of a slave-based economy. More importantly yet, a slave-based economy is not a profitable or sustainable economy. By the 1830s this fact was proving out in the South as the tariffs enacted to protect Northern fledgling industries, resulted in foreign tariffs in response, rendering southern cotton uncompetitive on the world market. A growing slave population requires a growing slave economy, which made slavery in the territories the only viable solution. In the 1840s and 1850s this was met with a growing abolitionist movement which increased the tension between the South and the North.

In this environment, the 1860 presidential election put Abraham Lincoln in the White House. He was not a friend to slavery, and fears of what policies might be implemented to further damage the southern slave economy became the final straw. South Carolina decided the only way out was to leave the union, and seceded on December 20, 1860. Mississippi, Florida, Alabama, Georgia, and Louisiana all seceded in January 1861, followed by Texas on February 1st. Union forces found themselves isolated in Fort Sumter in South Carolina. Lincoln was inaugurated on March 4th. On April 12 Confederate forces began shelling Fort Sumter and the Civil War began. In April, Virginia seceded, in May Arkansas, and North Carolina followed and finally Tennessee in June.

President Lincoln determined that the war was going to be very expensive, and federal revenues were going to shrink as duties and taxes from the southern ports were going to be taken by the new Confederate States. It became imperative to find new sources of federal income with which to finance the war. On July 4, 1861, Lincoln met with a joint session of Congress and asked them to create a tax on income. Congress obliged, and on August 5, 1861, the Revenue Act was passed and signed into law. This resulted in a 3% tax on all income in excess of $600 and 5% on all income in excess of $10,000. This resulted in only about 3% of Americans owing any income tax at all, and revenues fell far short of what was required. The tax was increased in 1864 to 5% for over $600, and 7.5% over $5,000, and 10% over $10,000. The income tax was altered a few more times and finally repealed by Congress in 1872.

Illinois attorney William M. Springer had filed his 1865 tax return showing $50,798 in income and $4,799 in tax due, which he refused to pay. In 1867, the IRS advertised some of Springer's property for sale to cover the tax liability. The property, one of which was his residence, finally sold in 1874, but Springer refused to vacate. The IRS filed a suit to have him ejected, and in response Springer challenged the constitutionality of the Revenue Act of 1864. Finally, in 1881 the Supreme Court upheld the IRS claim and said that the Revenue Act was constitutional and Springer's tax liability was not a direct tax in the meaning of Article I of the Constitution.

The Socialist Labor Party advocated for a new graduated income tax in 1887. Later, the Populist Party demanded a graduated income tax in its 1892 platform. In 1894, Congress reinstated the income tax with the Wilson-Gorman Tariff Act which included a 2% tax on incomes over $4,000.

In order to comply with the Act, Farmers' Loan & Trust Company told its shareholders that it would provide the IRS with the names of all members who would be liable to be taxed. Charles Pollock held 10 shares in the company, and sued to prevent the company from paying the tax. He hired Joseph Hodges Choate, an eminent Wall Street lawyer to argue his case. In its 1895 5 to 4 decision, the Supreme Court found in favor of Pollock. The court declared taxes on real estate, personal property, and income were direct taxes prohibited by Article I of the Constitution. This effectively killed the 1894 Act and the income tax provisions. Of course, the reversal of the court's view from 1881 did not return to William Springer the property sold by the IRS.

The Democratic Party took over the populist movement and made the income tax a platform plank. The Progressive Republicans also were in favor of an income tax as part of the AntiTrust and monopoly busting platform. So it was that in 1906 elected Nebraska Senator Norris Brown proposed what became the 16th amendment in 1911, which was ratified in 1913.

Article I, Section 8, Clause 1 gives the taxing power to the federal government and reads:
[Congress shall have the power] to lay and collect taxes, duties, imposts and excises, to pay the debt and provide for the common defense and general welfare of the United States; but all duties, imposts, and excises shall be uniform throughout the United States;
Duties: A tax levied on the import or export of goods.
Imposts: A tax, especially an import duty
Excise: taxes on manufacture, sale, or consumption of goods, or on licenses or corporate privileges.

So, it seems, duties, imposts, and excises are all taxes, just not on income. Duties, imposts, and excises are "indirect" taxes, meaning the person paying them can, and usually does, pass them on to other people. These indirect taxes, by the second part of this clause, must be the same throughout the United States.

Taxes on income would be a "direct tax", payable only by the person whose income is being taxed. Direct taxes are difficult to apply "uniformly" throughout the United States based on representation, a requirement of Article I. Accordingly, the 16th amendment did not "allow" income taxes, the federal government always had that power. What the 16th amendment did was to allow "direct taxes" on income without being apportioned to the states.

The real issue with taxation in the Constitution is that it is unlimited by anything other than the political capital to impose higher and higher taxes. This political capital runs out rather quickly when the taxes being imposed are "direct", but indirect taxes can be hidden and increased without much notice by the voter. There is no limit identified in Article I, Section 8, nor in the 16th amendment. This means that the federal government has the power to tax us without any limitations.

The Revenue Act of 1913 reinstated the now constitutional income tax with a 7-bracket tax table ranging from 1% to 7% graduated based on income. Americans began filing returns and paying taxes and very much noticing the amount of taxes being paid, which is to say that most Americans were blissfully unaware of the amount of import duties and excise taxes being passed on to them in products and services which far exceeded the minimal income tax they were now forced to notice each April 15th.

In 1916, with the coming of World War I, the tax tables went to 14 brackets, beginning at 2% and rising to 15% in the highest bracket. If voters didn't mind this, they surely noticed the 1917 increase which went to 21 brackets, hitting hard those earning $2,000 - $20,000 with rates graduating from 2% to 12%, while the top bracket paid 67%.

In 1916, the average tax return showed $14,414.19 in income with a tax due of $395.88 or about 2.75%. Only those Americans with very high incomes were required to file, with only 437,000 returns for a population of about 102 million or about 0.4%. By 1918, voters really noticed as the average return showed $3,598.87 income with $254.24 in taxes due. There were 4.4 million returns with a population of about 103 million or about 4.25% of Americans paying 7.06% tax.

By the end of the roaring 20s, incomes had risen, tax rates had fallen, and Americans had become used to the annual ritual of filing returns and paying 3-4% income tax. Then the stock market crashed, and the depression hit. Incomes fell from $4,425 in 1930 to $2,614 in 1932, the national debt went from $16.2 billion to $19.5 billion, Herbert Hoover raised taxes, and Franklin Roosevelt got elected.

FDR battled the depression with federal government programs, new agencies and policies of very questionable constitutionality. War raged in Europe, and assistance to the allies added to the financial burdens of Americans. By 1941, incomes were $1,200 lower than in 1932, taxes were $70 higher at 10.73% and the national debt was $49 billion, $29.9 billion more than the 1932 level. While this sounds like bad news, there is some good news. The Gross Domestic Product in 1929 was $105 billion, and while it fell to a low of $57 billion in 1933, by 1941 it had risen to $129 billion.

And then, Pearl Harbor, the day that will live in infamy. World War II propelled the U.S. economy into a boom that not only obliterated the depression issues, but would last with very few pauses into the next century. But the cost of prosecuting the war far out stripped the booming economy. By the end of the war in 1945, incomes were $2,403, taxes were $342, 14.22%. GDP had risen to $228 billion, but the national debt had ballooned to $258.7 billion. For the first time in history our debt was greater than GDP.

If voters had not much noticed the 2%, and 3% income tax rates, they were now painfully aware of the 10% to 15% rates. They were also very aware of a federal government spending two or three billion dollars above the twenty plus billion dollars in income tax revenue, never mind the revenues from all the other duties, imposts, and excises or indirect taxes.

Realizing that these high taxes could go higher because there was no limit constitutionally, in 1939, Maryland and Wyoming passed resolutions to an Article V convention to propose a repeal and replacement of the 16th amendment. Their plan was to limit taxes on income to 25%. Their applications read (*84 Cong. Rec. 3320, 1939*):

Resolved by the House of Delegates of Maryland, That the Congress of the United States be requested as follows: That application be, and it is hereby, made to the Congress of the United States of America to call a convention for the purpose of proposing the following article as an amendment to the Constitution of the United States:

"ARTICLE

"SECTION 1. The sixteenth amendment to the Constitution of the United States is hereby repealed.

"SEC. 2. The Congress shall have power to lay and collect taxes on income, from whatever source derived, without apportionment among the several States and without regard to any census of enumeration: Provided, that in no case shall the maximum rate of tax exceed 25 percent.

"SEC. 3. The maximum rate of any tax, duty, or excise which Congress may lay and collect with respect to the devolution or transfer of property, or any interest therein, upon or in contemplation of death, or by way of gift, shall in no case exceed 25 percent.

"SEC. 4. Sections 1 and 2 shall take effect at midnight on the 31st day of December, following the ratification of this article."

In 1940, Mississippi and Rhode Island made their applications. In 1941, Iowa, Maine, Massachusetts and Michigan filed applications. In 1943, Alabama, Arkansas, Delaware, Illinois, New Hampshire, Pennsylvania, and Wisconsin joined the movement. In 1944 Kentucky added their application bringing the total number of states to 16. Alabama, Arkansas, Iowa, and Wisconsin rescinded their applications in 1945, and Rhode Island rescinded theirs in 1949 reducing the number of states to 11. In 1951 Florida, Utah, and Kansas joined and Iowa reapplied and Kentucky rescinded making the total 14. Indiana, Georgia, and Virginia applied in 1952 while Massachusetts rescinded making the total 16. Louisiana applied and Maine rescinded in 1953. Louisiana rescinded in 1954.

Wyoming applied with another application in 1959, which I count as a duplicate for the purposes of repealing the 16th amendment. This application and the four that follow included other subjects with the repeal of the 16th amendment. These five are more commonly known as the "Liberty Amendment" and will be discussed later. Louisiana reapplied with a Liberty Amendment in 1960. Nevada and South Carolina applied with a Liberty Amendment in 1962. Finally in 1979 Arizona applied for a Liberty Amendment. With that, the number of states reached 19 for repeal of the 16th amendmont including the 5 Liberty Amendment applications, the highest it would ever get.

In 1992, Louisiana rescinded again. Utah followed in 2001, Arizona in 2003, Georgia, South Carolina, and Virginia in 2004, Wyoming in 2009, New Hampshire in 2010, Delaware in 2016 and finally Maryland and Nevada in 2017.

This leaves eight states with active applications to restrain the federal taxing authority.

Many of the states' applications included in the suggested amendment language a provision that in case of war the 25% limitation could be suspended such as this one from Alabama (89 Cong. Rec. 7523-24, 1943):

"Resolved by the Senate and House of Representatives of the State of Alabama, that application be, and it hereby is, made to the Congress of the United States of America to call a convention for the purpose of proposing the following article as an amendment to the Constitution of the United States:

"'ARTICLE

"'SECTION 1. The sixteenth article of amendment to the Constitution of the United States is hereby repealed.

"'SEC. 2. The Congress shall have power to lay and collect taxes on incomes, from whatever source derived, without apportionment among the several States, and without regard to any census or enumeration: Provided, that in no case shall the maximum rate of tax exceed 25 percent.

"'SEC. 3. The maximum rate of any tax, duty, or excise which Congress may lay and collect with respect to the devolution or transfer of property, or any interest therein, upon or in contemplation of or intended to take effect in possession or enjoyment at or after death, or by way of gift, shall in no case exceed 25 percent.

"'SEC. 4. The limitations upon the rates of said taxes contained in sections 2 and 3 shall, however, be subject to the qualification that in the event of a war in which the United States is engaged creating a grave national emergency requiring such action to avoid national disaster, the Congress by a vote of three-fourths of each House may for a period not exceeding 1 year increase beyond the limit, above prescribed the maximum rate of any such tax upon income subsequently accruing or received or with respect to subsequent devolutions or transfers of property, with like power, while the United States is actively engaged in such war, to repeat such action as often as such emergency may require.

"'SEC. 5. Sections 1 and 2 shall take effect at midnight on the 31st day of December following the ratification of this article. Nothing contained in this article shall affect the power of the United States after said date to collect any tax on incomes for any period ending on or prior to said 31st day of December laid in accordance with the terms of any law then in effect.

"'SEC. 6. Section 3 shall take effect at midnight on the last day of the sixth month following the ratification of this article. Nothing contained in this article shall affect the power of the United States to collect any tax on any devolution or transfer occurring prior to the taking effect of section 3, laid in accordance with the terms of any law then in effect;'

Later, other states sought to repeal the 16th amendment without replacement and restrict the federal government from competing in business activities, the liberty amendments. An example would be this one from Wyoming (*105 Cong. Rec. 3085-86, 1959):*

"Joint resolution proposing an amendment to the Constitution of the United States relative to abolishing personal income, estate, and gift taxes and prohibiting the United States Government from engaging in business in competition with its citizens

"Be it resolved by the Legislature of the State of Wyoming (the Senate and House of Representatives concurring herein), That the members of the 35th Legislature of the State of Wyoming respectfully requests the Congress of the United States to propose to the people an amendment to the Constitution of the United States or to call a convention for such

purpose, as provided by law, to add to the Constitution an article providing that:

" 'ARTICLE

"'SECTION 1. The Government of the United States shall not engage in any business, professional, commercial, financial, or industrial enterprise, except as specified in the Constitution.

"'SEC. 2. The Constitution or laws of any State, or the laws of the United States shall not be subject to the terms of any foreign or domestic agreement which would abrogate this amendment.

"'SEC. 3. The activities of the U.S. Government which violate the intent and purposes of this amendment shall, within a period of 3 years from the date of ratification of this amendment, be liquidated and the properties and facilities affected shall be sold.

"'SEC. 4. Three years after the ratification of this amendment the 16th article of amendments to the Constitution of the United States shall stand repealed and thereafter Congress shall not levy taxes on personal incomes, estates, and/or gifts;'

With all of this history behind us involving the unlimited nature of federal taxing authority and our national debt at nearly $33 trillion, which for the second time has climbed higher than our GDP, which is at $26 trillion, why are the state legislatures less interested in controlling the federal wallet than they were at the end of World War II? Perhaps it is the coercive use of seemingly unlimited federal funds. The federal money given to some states is far greater than the federal taxes paid by their residents, making it politically difficult for state legislatures to propose limitations on that federal revenue. Perhaps our federal government has grown so powerful, and our citizens have forgotten the intended limits on that power. Have we as a people come to accept an all-powerful federal government? Do too many Americans now believe that all money belongs to the government, and we just get to use it?

In any event, it is perplexing that state legislatures would join together in common cause between 1939 and 1944, only to fall apart and rescind their efforts in 1945. Then have a rebirth of belief from 1951 to 1979 only to have it die on the vine. Where is the will of the state legislatures? Where is the will of Americans to demand action of their states' legislature? Does anyone seriously entertain the notion that the Congress will pay down the national debt, reduce taxes and eliminate excess spending? If it is a lack of education and knowledge on the part of either the people or the legislatures, then by all means share this book!

This is clearly a time to unleash Article V. You can pressure your state legislators to support the use of this tool.

Below is a graph showing the number of states with new applications, rescissions and active applications by year:

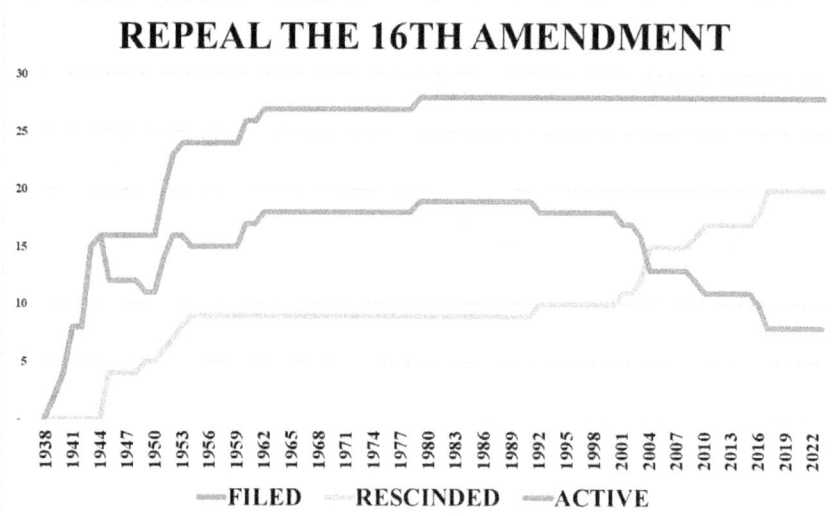

REVISE ARTICLE V

In 1920, the Speaker of the House of Representatives of the United States put before the House a resolution from Louisiana to call a convention. This is from the congressional record (*60 Cong. Rec. 31, 1920*):

The SPEAKER also laid before the House an application of the General Assembly of the State of Louisiana for the calling of a constitutional convention for the purpose of amending the Constitution of the United States so as to provide that all amendments to the Constitution of the United States shall be submitted to the qualified electors of the several States for ratification or rejection.

Having been unable to locate the actual resolution from the Louisiana General Assembly, we must be left to take the word of the Speaker that it exists.

But what does it say about the state of things? This would seek to change only the method of ratification from one of two methods to this single method. Remember, Article V says that Congress will determine if ratification is by state legislatures or by state conventions. This would seem to want to eliminate either choice and require ratification by the state's qualified electors. Presumably these electors would be those charged with electing the President of the United States. Should we be able to find the actual resolution, the reason for this application might be better understood.

Between 1953 and 1964, 14 more states submitted applications for a convention to propose an amendment to alter Article V. There were three versions of these applications. I'll refer to them as the Illinois version, the South Dakota version and the Arkansas version.

The Illinois version in 1953 was the first with this resolution (*109 Cong. Rec. 3788, 1963*):

"Be it resolved by the House of Representatives of the State of Illinois (the Senate concurring herein):

"That the General Assembly of the State of Illinois hereby respectfully makes application to the Congress of the United States to call a **convention for proposing an amendment to article V of the Constitution of the United States as such convention may deem appropriate to provide a clear absolute mode of proposing amendments to the Constitution by the sovereign States, and to make secure in the sovereign States their inherent power to amend the Constitution;**

The resolution goes on to ask that the convention be started in Constitution Hall in Independence Square in Philadelphia, beginning at 10am on the first Monday of the first December following transmission of applications by two-thirds of the several states. They then require that the states have equal votes and each is entitled to a single delegate and an alternate. Further, they say the convention is limited and restricted to the proposal of the specific amendment identified in the applications. That the issues of choosing officers of the convention, seating delegates, adjourning from day to day, selection of the place of meeting in the city, and the final adjournment of the convention are the total of their authority. The convention officers are responsible for a printed record of the proceedings and copies sent to the Senate, House, State Department, and each state.

Illinois seems to be wanting to use Article V of the Constitution to make an amendment to clarify the states' role and sovereignty in Article V. Further, in asking for this, they assert the sovereignty of the states by insisting on equal votes, and that the subject matter in the states' applications control and limit the scope of a convention. We will discuss sovereignty and control of the scope of the convention at the end of this chapter.

The South Dakota version was submitted in 1953 or 1955. The South Dakota House submitted an application in 1953 which was probably not valid until the South Dakota Senate submitted the same one in 1955 as a joint resolution. They wanted a third method of proposing amendments. Essentially adding that any state could propose an amendment by sending it to all other states and when 12 other states concurred in the proposed amendment it could then be transmitted to, voted on and ratified by three-quarters of the several states. A proposal of an amendment, a concurrence in a proposed amendment or a ratification could not be revoked. A proposed amendment must reach 12 concurrences within 7 years or it died. A proposed and concurred amendment must be ratified within 15 years of transmission or it died. The supreme court would settle controversies in the process.

They also resolved some very specific things in the application:
- That no precedent exists for calling or holding such a convention
- That absolute sovereign power of states to amend the constitution be acknowledged
- That absolute sovereign power of states to propose amendments be acknowledged
- That the states' absolute sovereign power will control the convention in scope of subject matter
- That state applications are the controlling element in convention scope
- That congress and the delegates to the convention have no power to act outside the scope
- The convention will be called and held in conformity with provisions and limitations
  a) Held in Philadelphia on the first Monday of the first December once two-thirds of states applications are received
  b) States have 3 delegates each with 1 vote, and exactly who the delegates shall be
  c) Limited to proposing the identified amendment to Article V
  d) Convention delegates will choose the convention officers, rules, seating of delegates, daily adjournment, place of meeting, and final adjournment
  e) Transcript of the convention will be made and placed in the Library of Congress

Unlike Illinois, who wanted to establish state control of the convention by their amendment, South Dakota wants a third method of proposing amendments. However, just like Illinois in 1953, South Dakota is establishing that the sovereign states are in control of the conventions' proceedings, and that those proceedings are limited by the specification contained in the applications.

In 1955, Texas and Georgia submitted applications identical to that of South Dakota. In 1956, Michigan and Illinois did the same. In 1957 Idaho and Indiana joined the other states.

In 1963, Arkansas made an application to revise Article V, but in a very different way. Arkansas also proposed a third method of proposing amendments while keeping the two-thirds vote of both houses of Congress and application of two-thirds of the several states for a convention. In their third method, two-thirds of the state legislatures could submit identical language for an amendment and once certified by the President of the Senate and the Speaker of the House was deemed proposed. With no further action the proposed amendment could be ratified by three-quarters of the state legislatures.

Florida, Idaho, Illinois, Missouri, Oklahoma, South Carolina, South Dakota, Texas, and Wyoming all submitted identical applications to Arkansas. In 1964 Virginia added its application to the list.

In these applications, there is none of the uncertainty about sovereignty shown in the Illinois and South Dakota applications. It's just straight forward telling Congress what Arkansas, a sovereign state, wants them to do, and the expectation that they will do it under the provisions of Article V.

From 1964 to 1992 this is where matters stood with regard to revising Article V and the amendment process. Fifteen states had twenty open applications to modify Article V. Basically, there were four versions of this application:the non-specific Louisiana resolution from 1920; the original Illinois application from 1953;the South Dakota application from 1955 with identical applications from six other states;and the Arkansas application from 1963 and identical ones from ten other states.

In 1992, Louisiana rescinded all of its prior applications for Article V conventions regardless of subject matter. Idaho did the same in 2000, Georgia, South Carolina, and Virginia followed in 2004, Oklahoma and Wyoming in 2009, South Dakota in 2010, Texas in 2017, and Illinois in 2022. This leaves today two states Michigan and Indiana with the South Dakota application active and Arkansas, Florida, and Missouri with the Arkansas application still active.

In 2011, North Dakota filed an application to revise Article V. I've included the entire resolution here because it identifies the same concerns of sovereignty and control as did the Illinois and South Dakota applications, which were missing from the Arkansas application *(158 Cong. Rec. H3805 (daily ed. May 31, 2011).*

*A concurrent resolution urging Congress to **call a convention for the sole purpose of proposing an amendment to the Constitution of the United States to avoid a "runaway convention".***

*WHEREAS, experience has shown that the **safeguards in the United States Constitution**, as currently interpreted, **may not be sufficiently clear** to limit a Constitutional Convention to the specific subject for which that convention was called and thereby avoid a "runaway convention" where other matters may be considered; and*

*WHEREAS, **James Madison**, who is known as the "Father of the Constitution", **believed that Article V of the Constitution gave and should give this protection**; and*

WHEREAS, those who framed and adopted the Constitution included a provision by which state legislatures may require Congress to call a convention for proposing amendments as a way to amend the United States Constitution; and

*WHEREAS, the North Dakota Legislative Assembly accordingly **makes application to Congress for the calling of a convention for proposing an amendment to the Constitution imposing certain rules of fiscal discipline, providing for legislative transparency, and preventing unfunded mandates by the federal government;***

NOW, THEREFORE, BE IT RESOLVED BY THE HOUSE OF REPRESENTATIVES OF NORTH DAKOTA, THE SENATE CONCURRING THEREIN:

BE IT FURTHER RESOLVED, that the North Dakota Legislative Assembly makes the following application:

*Section 1. **The North Dakota legislative assembly makes an application to the Congress of the United States pursuant to Article V of the Constitution of the United States to call an Article V Amendment Convention for the sole purpose of voting to propose or voting not to propose the following specific amendment to the Constitution of the United States**:*

"Article_____. The Congress, on Application of the Legislatures of two-thirds of the several States, which all contain an identical Amendment, shall call a Convention solely to decide whether to propose that specific Amendment to the States, which if proposed shall be valid to all intents and purposes as part of the Constitution when ratified pursuant to Article V."

Section 2. For the purpose of determining whether the required two-thirds of the legislatures of the several states have applied for a convention, this application may be counted and considered valid only in conjunction with qualifying applications of other states that contain the identical text of the specific amendment contained in this application and whose application requires that the sole purpose of the convention is to decide whether to propose, or not to propose this specific amendment.

Section 3. This concurrent resolution is revoked and withdrawn, nullified, and superseded to the same effect as if it had never been passed, and retroactive to the date of passage, if it is used to conduct a convention that votes to propose any amendment other than the specific text of the amendment contained in Section 1.

Section 4. Each delegate selected to represent North Dakota at a convention that Congress calls under this resolution shall take an oath, enforceable under this state's law, to abide by and act according to the limits imposed by this resolution on the purpose of the convention.

Section 5. Any delegate selected to represent North Dakota at a convention that Congress calls under this resolution does not have authority to consider or approve any other amendment but the one contained in this application. Any vote taken in violation of this limitation is null and void, and any delegate who so votes does not have any authority to represent this state on any matter at the convention.

Section 6. This application is valid if two-thirds of the states make a qualifying application within seven years of its referral for ratification to the states by Congress under the provisions of Article V.

Section 7. This application is null and void if Congress, within 90 days of receipt of qualifying applications from two-thirds of the states, proposes and refers to the ratification by the several states under the procedures outlined in Article V of the Constitution, the same exact text of the amendment contained in this application.

Section 8. That the secretary of state forward copies of this application within 30 days of its passage to the Speaker of the United States House of Representatives, the Clerk of the United States House of Representatives, the President of the United States Senate, the Secretary of the United States Senate, every member of the North Dakota Congressional Delegation, and the presiding officers of each house of the legislatures of the several states.

Clearly, the legislature of North Dakota in 2011 was multi-tasking. Here's what they asked for:
1. Call a convention to propose an amendment to avoid a "runaway convention".
2. Call a convention to propose an amendment to impose certain rules of fiscal discipline, providing for legislative transparency, and preventing unfunded mandates by the federal government.
3. Call a convention to propose a specific amendment to revise Article V of the Constitution.
   a) Only count this application with states submitting identical amendment language
   b) Rescinds the entire resolution if used to count with other states applications other than the amendment above
   c) Requires North Dakota delegates to take an oath to act within the limits of this resolution
   d) No North Dakota delegate may consider any other proposed amendment
   e) This application expires if the two-thirds threshold is not met within seven years
   f) This application is void if Congress proposes the amendment

It seems that North Dakota has made three applications in one resolution.

The first application seems to be made without the concerns of the second or the stipulations that limit the third. If the call to amend Article V to prevent a "runaway convention" is made without concerns, then why express the concerns as a prelude to the second call? If the legislature had read Federalist 40, perhaps they would be less afraid of a "runaway convention", because Madison clearly said the Constitutional Convention was not a runaway. Further, the concept that the Constitutional Convention was a runaway convention is an attempt at fear mongering. This was first used by the Anti-Federalists during the ratifying conventions. This same fear mongering is being used today by the left and some misinformed groups on the right. But more on this later.

The concern identified as the justification for the second call seems to be that constitutional safeguards are not sufficiently clear, even though James Madison felt they were. Without doubt, our Constitution has been very poorly interpreted by the Supreme Court over the last 130 years. Article V is the vehicle designed by the founders to remedy that very thing. The best example of the use of this remedy is the 11th Amendment itself. The Supreme Court heard the appeal of Chisholm v. Georgia and ruled for Chisholm. Chisholm, a resident of South Carolina, had sued Georgia for non-payment of debts related to supplies provided to Georgia during the Revolutionary War. The Georgia high court found against Chisholm and Georgia did not pay the debt. Chisholm appealed to the Supreme Court and won there. Congress proposed the 11th amendment to "clarify" the jurisdiction of the Supreme Court to not include suits by residents of another state or a foreign country against any state. So, the 11th amendment, once ratified, nullified the finding of the Supreme Court. Could other amendments be proposed to once again provide clarity on the interpretation of the constitution by the Supreme Court and return us to the certainty that James Madison enjoyed? Perhaps North Dakota is referring to correcting some of the Supreme Court mis-defining terms in the Constitution resulting in federal overreach in some very specific areas: fiscal discipline, transparency, and unfunded mandates.

It also seems that the restrictions identified only apply to the call for a convention to propose the specific amendment to Article V laid out in the third call. If so, do they not intend these restrictions to apply to a convention called to propose amendments on the other two subjects? If the restrictions apply to all three calls, then clarification is needed.

In any event, applications to revise Article V which are active now stand at five.

In 2014, Supreme Court justice Antonin Scalia was asked how he felt about a Convention to amend the constitution. In his answer, he expressed concerns about an unlimited convention because who knows what could happen. But he went on to say that if there were an amendment he would like, it would be to amend Article V to make amending the Constitution easier. He opined that it takes 38 states to ratify an amendment, but only 13 to stop it. Further, if you consider the populations of the 13 smallest states, an amendment could be stopped by about 2 percent of the population. He said, "It ought to be hard to amend the Constitution but not that hard."

Let's do the math. In the 2020 census, the total population of the 13 smallest states was 14,618,613, and the total population of all 50 states was 330,759,736. The 13 smallest states constitute 4.4% of all 50. Scalia's 2 percent estimate was off a little, but not much. Maybe if we consider that only 51% of those states' legislators would have to vote to not ratify, that would only represent half of the population of those states. So, half of 4.4% would be 2.2%, and Scalia's math was dead on.

The common theme of all 22 of these applications is to both render amending the constitution by the states easier and to assure that the sovereign states are in control of the process.

Let's understand state sovereignty. In 1776, the thirteen British Colonies each declared their independence from Great Britain. They each had already formed or soon would form their own independent governments, making them sovereign nations. By 1786, those thirteen sovereign nations had become united in a loose confederation with a central congress as a governing body. That confederation and governing body was not fulfilling the needs of the union. Accordingly, they sent delegates to a convention in Annapolis, Maryland to discuss this problem. Only five sets of delegates showed up, and they decided to convene again in Philadelphia and invited all thirteen to send delegates, "**to devise such further provisions as shall appear to them necessary to render the constitution of the Federal Government adequate to the exigencies of the Union**" (Proceedings and Report of the Commissioners at Annapolis Maryland, 1786).

They did so, and the delegates to the Philadelphia convention proposed the Constitution to accomplish that purpose. The delegates sent their recommendation to each of the sovereign nations' legislatures and to the Congress. Congress unanimously voted to submit it to the states for ratification, lending credibility to the convention's results. Twelve of the sovereign states gave credibility to the convention and the proposed constitution by calling ratifying conventions, and Rhode Island simply held a popular vote. In the end, all thirteen sovereign states and all thirty-seven that have since joined the union have shared their sovereignty in the specific powers identified in the constitution, and retained all other sovereign powers to themselves. Certainly, they created this constitution with their sovereign powers and retain the sovereign power to amend or even nullify or replace it. However, a convention called under Article V of the constitution would necessarily be limited to amending it. Replacing or nullifying would be done outside of the provisions within the constitution, such as the Convention of the Northeastern states to debate secession over the war of 1812 or the Convention to establish the confederacy in 1861. The fact that the Northeastern secession did not happen, and the confederacy was dissolved by force does not nullify the sovereignty of the states. After all, the states which seceded in 1861 under their own sovereignty also rejoined the union under their own sovereignty.

Remember the language of Article V, "upon application of two-thirds of the several states, **Congress SHALL** call a convention for proposing amendments". Clearly, the states are in control because Congress is obliged by the word SHALL to do what they have asked. If two-thirds of the states have asked for the same thing, say a convention for proposing amendments either unlimited or limited to specific subjects, or a specific amendment, then that is what binds Congress. Asking for the convention to be initiated at Constitution Hall is a nice symbolic touch but has no relevance as to who is in charge of the convention. The precedent of the 40 plus Conventions of States should be enough to ensure one state one vote, the convention delegates control over officers, rules, and adjournment, after all it is a meeting, whose attendees are the commissioners of equal sovereigns. The states are at a clear disadvantage to the U. S. Congress in the ability to propose an amendment. This can be resolved by unleashing Article V.

The graph below shows the number of states with new applications, rescissions and active applications by year:

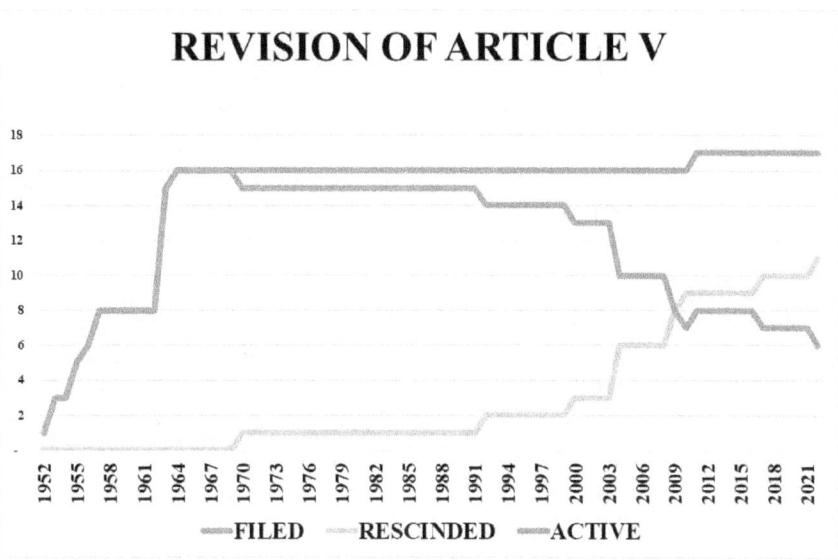

BALANCED BUDGET AMENDMENT

During his administration, Andrew Jackson did something no one since has been able to accomplish. On January 8, 1835, he paid off the national debt. The only time in American history when the debt was zero. Since then, our federal government has spent $33 trillion more than they have taken in from all sources.

Does anyone understand what a trillion is? Consider this, if you spent $10,000 per day for 100 days, you would have spent $1 million. 100 Days is 0.267 years. If you continued to spend $10,000 per day, it would take 267 years to spend $1 billion. Which means that it would take 267,000 years at $10,000 per day to spend $1 trillion.

From January 8, 1835, the day Jackson made us debt free, to September 30, 2021, the end of the federal government fiscal year, is 68,201 days. $28,428,920,000,000, the 2021 national debt, divided by 68,201 is $416,840,222.28 per day. That's nearly $417 million per day MORE THAN all the income of the federal government for that same time frame.

At what point do we consider that amount to be "a lot"? Generally, we decide what is a lot, by comparing it to what we understand, and we understand what we have and what we earn. For example, someone with $1 million in the bank and earning $400 thousand a year may consider $10,000 insignificant, whereas someone with $1,200 in the bank and earning $36 thousand a year, it is quite significant.

Our national income is what we call the Gross Domestic Product, the value of all goods and services produced in the entire country for a given year. In 1929, the last year of the roaring 20s, our GDP was $105 billion, and our national debt was $16.9 billion or about 16%. In 1920 it had been about 39%, so 16% felt pretty good. But then, the depression hit and by 1941 the debt was back to 38%. If that wasn't bad enough, the U.S. entered World War II, and the debt skyrocketed. In 1946, the debt was 118% of GDP. After World War II, the economy boomed and GDP went from $250 billion in 1947 to $474 billion in 1957, an 89% increase. But the debt went from $258 billion to $270 billion a 4.6% increase, and it was still 57% of GDP.

The Korean War, the Cold War, the Space Race, Vietnam, the Great Society, OPEC, and the Arms Race kept American and the world mesmerized for the next 25 years. All of these became reasons for the federal government to continue deficit spending. Between 1957 and 1983 the national debt had gone from $270 billion to $1,377 billion, more than a fivefold increase. But GDP had also ballooned from $474 billion to $3,634 billion, a seven-fold increase. More importantly, the debt was now only 38% of GDP, back to the 1920 level.

While the debt to GDP ratio was improving, it was still true that more years than not, the federal government ran a deficit. Americans continue to question why they had to balance their household budget, but the federal government did not. Many state legislatures are required to balance their budgets as well. Consequently, state legislatures began to question why the federal government was not required to balance their budget.

In 1957, Indiana submitted the first application for an Article V convention to propose a balanced budget amendment. They suggested the following amendment (*103 Cong. Rec. 6475-76, 1957*):

On or before the 15th day after the beginning of each regular session of the Congress, the President shall transmit to the Congress a budget which shall set forth his estimates of the receipts of the Government, other than trust funds, during the ensuing fiscal year under the laws then existing and his recommendations with respect to expenditures to be made from funds other than trust funds during such ensuing fiscal year, which shall not exceed such estimate of receipts. If the Congress shall authorize expenditures to be made during such ensuing fiscal year in excess of such estimated receipts, it shall not adjourn for more than 3 days at a time until action has been taken necessary to balance the budget for such ensuing fiscal year. In case of war or other grave national emergency, if the President shall so recommend, the Congress by a vote of three-fourths of all the Members of each House may suspend the foregoing provisions for balancing the budget for periods, either successive or otherwise, not exceeding 1 year each.

Their resolution went on to stipulate many of the concerns and conditions around state sovereignty that were present in the Revision of Article V applications.

Wyoming submitted their application for a convention to propose a balanced budget amendment in 1961 without the many stipulations and conditions and without specifying amendment language. Virginia submitted an application in 1973 which did not contain specific amendment language, but did have the stipulations and conditions. In 1975, Alabama, Louisiana, and Mississippi submitted applications very similar to Virginia's. In 1976, seven more states joined in the call for a balanced budget amendment convention. In 1977, a group of state legislators started the Balanced Budget Amendment Task Force (BBATF) to work with other states to submit applications. More states continued to join the call, five in 1977, two in 1978, ten in 1979 and one each in 1982 and 1983. This brought the total number of applications for a balanced budget amendment to 32, only two states short of the threshold which would require congress to act.

All movement stalled for the next five years. Then in 1988, Florida, in what sounds like a fit of frustration with Congress and other states who had not yet submitted a balanced budget application, rescinded their application. I've included the entire resolution here to show the level of frustration which the Florida legislature is venting (*134 Cong. Rec. 15,363, 1988*)

"Senate Memorial No. 302

"Whereas, the people of the State of Florida have adopted, as a provision of their state constitution, the requirement that the state government operate on the basis of a balanced budget, and that requirement has proved of great benefit to the state, and

"Whereas, in 1976, responding to national concern over a public debt which was then in excess of $300 billion and the existence of a $43 billion federal deficit, the Florida Legislature made application to the Congress of the United States to call a constitutional convention to propose an amendment to the Constitution of the United States requiring a balanced federal budget, and

"Whereas, the national debt in 1986 exceeded $1 trillion, and the estimated 1987 deficit is now approximately $173.2 billion, and

"Whereas, what was national concern in 1976 has, in 1988, become a national crisis, and

"Whereas, this condition of our national fiscal policy threatens the security of our nation, and

"Whereas, the threat to the security of our nation has become so imminent that we can no longer afford the time and expense of a constitutional convention to propose and debate a solution to the crisis that is self-evident, and

"Whereas, Article V of the Constitution of the United States provides for the proposal of amendments to the Constitution of the United States by two-thirds concurrence of the members of both Houses of Congress, and

"Whereas, we should each and every one demand of our U.S. Senators and Congressmen that such an amendment be introduced in both houses of the Congress and that the elected Florida delegation lead the fight to bring about the proposal of this critically important constitutional amendment; Now, therefore, be it

"Resolved by the Legislature of the State of Florida, That the Congress of the United States is urged to adopt, without delay, a joint resolution providing for an amendment to the Constitution of the United States that requires the federal budget to be in balance except under specified emergency conditions.

"Be it further resolved, That the Congress of the United States is urged to take appropriate and immediate action to continue to bring the federal budget into balance and to cause the reduction of the outstanding national debt in the foreseeable future.

"Be it further resolved, that this memorial supersedes all previous memorials applying to the Congress of the United States to call a convention to propose an amendment to the Constitution of the United States to require a balanced federal budget, including Senate Memorial No. 234 and House Memorial No. 2801, both passed in 1976, and that such previous memorials are hereby revoked and withdrawn.

While these are very pointed statements about the situation with the federal deficit and national debt, why throw in the towel? Why, when the power of the states to act is clearly laid out in Article V, and 32 have done so, would the Florida legislature give up? Why not spend the effort to lobby the other 18 states to submit applications and join in the fight to reign in the spending of the federal government? Did the 1988 Florida legislature really believe that Congress will ever propose an amendment to constrain their ability to spend?

In defense of Congress, well, a few members anyway, there was some support for the concept of a balanced budget. On January 15, 1979, Texas representative Phill Gramm (R), introduced HJR 39 to propose a balanced budget. He had 14 co-sponsors from seven states. It was referred to the Judiciary committee and quickly forgotten. In August of 1982, representative Paul Simon (D – IL) introduced his proposed balanced budget amendment which ultimately went to the sub-committee on Monopolies and Commercial Law to die. Ken Kramer (R – CO) submitted his with 32 co-sponsors which died in the sub-committee on Civil and Constitutional Rights. This happened over and over with the same result. Then in February 1993, now Senator Phill Gramm and 55 other senators actually got a floor vote in the Senate for an amendment proposal. That vote was 63 yea, 37 nay. The requirement being 67, it failed.

The high-water mark came in 1995. Joe Barton (R – TX) submitted HJR 1 on January 4, 1995, with 177 co-sponsors from 40 states. Remember, in order to propose an amendment requires 2/3 vote of both the House and the Senate. The House passed the proposed amendment on January 26th, with a vote of 300 yeas, 132 nay, the required 2/3 being 288. The resolution moved to the senate where the required 2/3 would be 67 yeas. The Senate vote on March 2nd, was 65 yeas, 35 nay, failed by only 2 votes. Senator Robert Dole (R – KS), wishing to change his vote from nay to yea, made a motion to reconsider the resolution. The motion laid on the table until June 4th when the motion to reconsider was agreed to by unanimous consent. The new vote was taken on June 6th where it once again failed with 64 yea and 35 nay votes. Senator Dole went from N to Y, Senator Exon (D – NE) changed his vote from Y to N offsetting Dole's change. Senator Packwood (R – OR) was absent, reducing the yeas by one, and Senator Pell (D – RI) changed from N to present.

Senator Orin Hatch (R – UT) introduced an amendment in 1997 which got a floor vote of 66 yeas, 34 nay, but being one vote short of the 67 it did not move to the House. Almost every year since, there has been an amendment introduced in one or both chambers to no avail.

Alabama then rescinded their application in 1990 without any explanation in their resolution. Between 1992 and 2009, Louisiana, Idaho, Oregon, North Dakota, Utah, Arizona, Georgia, South Carolina, Virginia, Oklahoma, and Wyoming all made rescissions of all their applications for Article V conventions which included the balanced budget. This reduced the number of active applications to 19.

While all of these states were busy rescinding their applications for a convention, and Congress was busy ignoring proposed amendments, the economy continued to grow and deficit spending got worse and the national debt went much higher. From 1984, the GDP went from $4,038 billion to $14,992 billion, an increase of nearly four times. The national debt had gone from $1,572 billion to $13,561 growing more than eight times. This moved the debt to GDP ratio from the seemingly acceptable 39% back to a very unacceptable 90%.

If the 1988 Florida legislature had thrown in the towel, the 2010 legislature picked it up, dusted it off, and made a new application for a convention to propose a balanced budget amendment. However, that same year New Hampshire, South Dakota, and Tennessee all made rescissions of their active applications, including the balanced budget one. In 2016 Delaware, and in 2017, Maryland, Nevada, and New Mexico joined by Colorado made mass rescissions including their balanced budget application.

Meanwhile, the GDP continued to grow, but the federal government continued to have higher and higher deficits and the debt grew much faster than the economy. Between 2010 and 2022, the GDP went from $15,543 billion to $26,140 billion, a 68% increase. The debt doubled from $14,790 billion to $30,929 billion. For the second time in history, the national debt is higher than the GDP at 118%, the same as in 1946.

Even though many states had rescinded all of their active applications, Arizona 2017, Georgia 2014, Louisiana 2014, New Hampshire 2012, South Dakota 2015, Tennessee 2014, and Wyoming 2017 all sent in new applications for a balanced budget convention. Alabama in 1990 and Utah in 2001 had rescinded their balance budget applications specifically, but Alabama in 2011 and Utah in 2015 submitted new applications.

States that had not participated in the movement in the 1970s also began to submit applications for a balanced budget convention. These are Ohio 2013, Michigan 2014, North Dakota 2015, West Virginia 2016, and Wisconsin 2017. It should also be noted that Texas made a mass rescission of their active applications in 2017, excluding their 1977 balanced budget application which remains active.

With all of the applying, rescinding and reapplying, here's where we are. Having reached a high of 32 states in 1983, and a low of 17 states in 2010, we have done a stutter step back up to 26 states as of 2022.

It should be noted that when Arizona made its application for a balanced budget convention, it made a second resolution as well. This was done with the advocacy of the BBATF members. The second resolution called for a Convention of States to plan for an Article V Convention to propose a balanced budget amendment. This called for a planning committee made up of members of the Arizona legislature, and an invitation to all 50 state legislatures to attend the planning convention in Phoenix in September of 2017.

That convention was held with 19 states sending official delegates and another 3 states had unofficial observers.

Here are the states and number of assigned and attended delegates:

STATE	DELGATES	ALTERNATES	ATTENDED
Alabama	1		1
Arizona	7	7	9
Georgia	4		3
Idaho	10		9
Indiana	4		4
Iowa	2	1	3
Kansas	1		1
Kentucky	1		1
Michigan	1		1
Minnesota	5		5
Misouri	1		1
New Hampshir	7		6
Oklahoma	8	1	7
South Carolina	2		2
South Dakota	3		3
Tennessee	7		7
Utah	6	2	5
West Virginia	1		1
Wyoming	5		3
TOTAL	76	11	72

The convention was divided into a Rules Committee and a Planning Committee.

A synopsis of the product of the Rules Committee is as follows:
1. Produced a model set of rules for an Article V convention to propose a BBA. Some components of the set of model rules were as follows:
    a. The Article V convention shall be limited in scope to the balanced budget amendment. Governing rules provide for appropriate order and conduct during a BBA Article V convention which include, but are not limited to, the following:
        i. Duties of the officers.

ii. A quorum is a majority of the states in attendance.

iii. Each state shall be given only one vote, as has been the precedent in all preceding state conventions.

iv. Order of business and names of committees.

v. The cost of the convention to be divided equally among the states in attendance.

A synopsis of the Planning Committee is as follows:

1. Recommendations for protecting the integrity of an Article V Convention.

    a. Non-delegates should not be permitted on the Chamber Floor, Members' Lounge, etc. and should only be permitted in public areas.

    b. Any interaction of Convention leadership and staff with non-delegate individuals or organizations that pertains to Convention business or process should be strictly prohibited, with the exception of the press.

    c. Convention communications should only include official activities.

    d. States should consider extending their ethics restrictions (i.e. lobbying, food, gifts, etc.) to delegates serving within a convention, in addition to any ethics standards imposed by Convention rules.

2. Sub-Committee on Delegates and Correspondence reported the following:

    a. In anticipation of the call for a convention for proposing amendments, states are strongly encouraged to enact delegate selection legislation at the earliest opportunity.

    b. The Phoenix Correspondence Commission (PCC) was created. The PCC will consist of commissioners appointed by the states to carry out the following functions to organize a convention for proposing amendments:

    i. Creating a single point of contact to act as a liaison with Congress.

    ii. Track all applications for a convention for proposing amendments.

    iii. Create a process to suggest to Congress a time and place for a convention for proposing amendments.

    iv. Provide a process for legal representation, if necessary.

v. Perform tasks as needed to organize the convention.

vi. Each state is strongly encouraged to appoint a commissioner to the PCC to communicate on all matters associated with a convention for proposing amendments with any or all of the following:

1. State Legislators,
2. United States Citizens,
3. Convention Organizers,
4. State Congressional Delegations,
5. Congress.
6. The members of the PCC will be comprised of one member appointed from each delegation present at this Arizona Balanced Budget Amendment Planning Convention, until such time as each commissioner's state formally appoints a commissioner to the PCC or declines to do the same.

Of course, there is no reason that these rules and plans could not be used for an Article V convention on any subject, should it be called. The complete rules package is in appendix 4.

It was also noted in the conventions report to Congress, that at no time did the delegates stray from or exceed the purpose and subject specified in the invitation. That is to say it did not "run-away".

While none of the above is binding, it does demonstrate that at least 19 states can appoint delegates who know the purpose of their convention and adhere to that purpose.

In addition to the BBATF, there is another group working for a balanced budget amendment. This is the Compact for America organization. They have a slightly different process in mind. They propose an initial step of an Interstate Compact in order to control the convention. Generally, they are targeting 38 states to join the compact. Once the compact is in place, applications would be made to congress, the convention would be called, and held in a couple of days according to the compact agreement. The amendment would then be proposed and ratified in fairly short order. This process began in 2014, and there are only five states in the compact so far.

Congress has also renewed its efforts to propose a balanced budget amendment. In 2011, two resolutions were considered and failed in the Senate. Senator Orin Hatch (R – UT) introduced his amendment proposal in March, 2011, which was voted down on December 14, 2011 with a vote of 47 yea, 53 nay. Senator Mark Udall (D – CO) introduced his proposed amendment in August, 2011 which was voted down the same day as Senator Hatch's resolution. The Udall vote was worse with 21 yeas, 79 nay. The Udall proposal would have prevented congress from reducing taxes on people earning over $1 million per year.

That same year Bob Goodlatte (R – VA) introduced a resolution in the House which ultimately failed in November with a vote of 261 yeas to 165 nay. Goodlatte reintroduced his proposal in 2017, once again achieving a floor vote but failing with 233 yeas, 184 nay.

Every year there is at least one resolution for a balanced budget amendment submitted in one or both chambers of congress. The last vote in the House was in 2017, and the last in the Senate was in 2011. The votes are getting worse every time, so it must be up to the state legislatures to force the issue.

If you are averse to being $33 trillion in debt, tell your state legislator to unleash Article V.

Below is a graph showing the number of states with new applications, rescissions, and active applications by year:

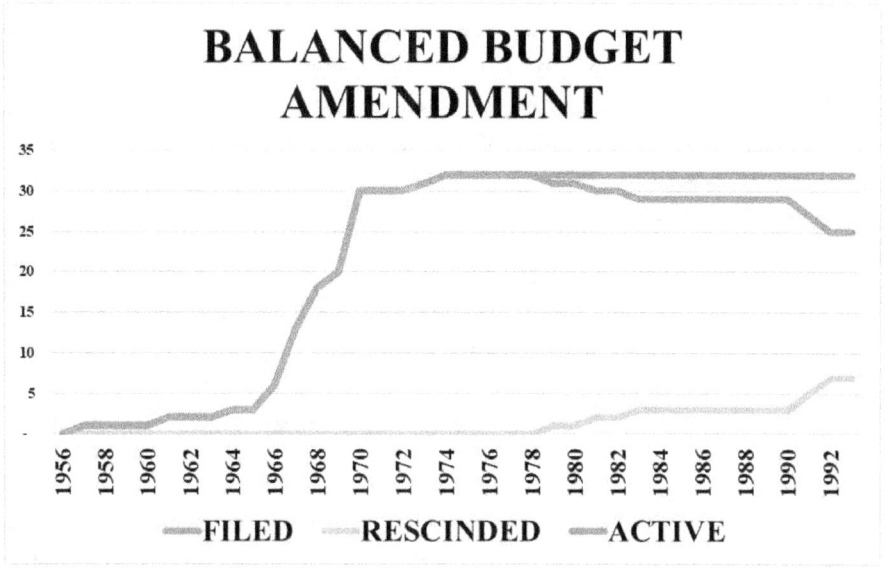

APPORTIONMENT AMENDMENT

It was the summer of 1957. At the time of the early civil rights movement, school segregation had been deemed unconstitutional in Brown v Board of Education in 1955, and integration was underway. Congress was working on the Civil Rights Act of 1957. In Macon County, Alabama, Charles B. Gomillion was working with his Tuskegee Civic Association to register as many black voters as they could.

Gomillion had been home-schooled by his mother who had instilled in him the value of education. After saving for a few years, he was able to afford to enroll in Paine High School in Augusta, Georgia, and eventually Paine College where he finally received his bachelor's degree at the age of 28. He became a faculty member at Tuskegee Institute in Tuskegee, Alabama, as well as continuing his education, ultimately receiving his Doctorate in Sociology from Ohio State University in 1959.

Samuel Englehardt was a planter and ginner from Shorter, Alabama. He had a degree from Washington and Lee University and had been a state representative from Macon County from 1950 to 1954, and a state senator from 1954 to 1958. He was known for his strong stand on segregation, and was the chairman of the State Democratic Executive Committee.

In 1957, the population of Tuskegee in Macon County, Alabama, was about 6,700 with about 5,300 being black. The entire population of Tuskegee was inside the city limits which comprised a 4-mile square. There were about 600 whites registered to vote, and with Gomillion's voter registration drive, the number of black voters had risen to 410. Senator Englehardt authored, introduced, and got passed by the Alabama legislature the Tuskegee Gerrymandering Act of 1957 (Act 140). This Act transformed the shape of Tuskegee from the 4-sided square into a 28-sided shape that resulted in less than a dozen of the 410 registered black voters inside the city limits. Clearly, this had the effect intended by Englehardt on the composition of the Tuskegee city council.

Gomillion organized a protest and boycott of white businesses which was supported by nearly all of the blacks of Tuskegee. He and others filed a lawsuit in Federal District Court, naming Mayor Phillip Lightfoot as the defendant, claiming that the Act was discriminatory in its purpose under the due process and equal protection clause of the 14th amendment of the U.S. Constitution.

Judge Frank M. Johnson of the U.S. District Court for the Middle District of Alabama in Montgomery dismissed the case, ruling that the state had the right to draw boundaries however it liked. This ruling was upheld by the Fifth Circuit Court in New Orleans on appeal. Gomillion enlisted the NAACP and its lawyers to take the case to the Supreme Court. In 1960, the Supreme Court found in favor of Gomillion, overturning the lower courts rulings. In the courts' ruling, Justice Frankfurter cited the 15th amendment saying that Act 140 denied the right to vote "on account of race, color or previous condition of servitude". Justice Whittaker concurred with the decision but not the 15th amendment, he cited the 14th equal protection clause as the correct ruling. The case was returned to the District Court and Act 140 was reversed and the original square shape was returned to Tuskegee in 1961.

Remember one of the key concepts in the Constitution is that of shared sovereignty. Primacy was granted by the sovereign states to the federal government on certain subjects. The 14th amendment granted primacy to the federal government in guaranteeing that citizens receive due process and equal protection of the law in state law as well as federal law. The 15th amendment granted primacy to the federal government in protecting every citizen's right to vote regardless of race, color or previous condition of servitude. Does that primacy extend to how jurisdictional lines are drawn? Clearly, Act 140 in 1957 drew lines that would remove the right of blacks to vote in city elections or measures. In Colegrove v. Green, 1946, the Supreme Court said that apportionment was a political thicket into which the judiciary should not intrude. Taking Colegrove and Gomillion together, it would seem that the federal government has no role in the drawing of political jurisdictions unless there is a clear violation of due process, equal protection or the right to vote.

In Baker v. Carr in 1962, the Supreme Court forced the Tennessee legislature to reapportion itself on the basis of population. Tennessee had not redistricted its state legislative districts since 1901 despite their state constitution requiring that they do so. Consequently, Shelby County, which includes the city of Memphis, had increased substantially in population without a likely increase in state representation in the legislature. Of course, this was true of nearly every urban area in the country over the first half of the 20th century. In the Baker opinion, the court cited Gomillion as a precedent, thus formalizing the reversal of the finding in Colegrove. Later in Reynolds v. Sims in 1964, where Alabama was in the same position as Tennessee, the court held that "legislators represent people, not trees or acres", Baker was cited as precedent. This solidified the concept of "one man one vote", meaning that any legislative body should have population proportionate representation. The ruling required that both houses of a state with a bicameral legislature must be apportioned based on population. John Marshall Harlan II dissented, arguing that each state should be allowed to determine the composition of their legislature as this lies outside the reach of the Supreme Court. Perhaps the better argument is the example of the US House being apportioned on population while the US Senate is based on one state, one vote, not population. Why would a state not have constituent interests which are not population based but deserve representation?

In response to the decision in Reynolds v. Sims, Senator Everett Dirksen (R), Illinois, objected to the population being the sole consideration in representation. He cited the fact that the huge population of Chicago would dictate to all of the rural areas of Illinois. He began to propose an amendment allowing one house of a state legislature to be based on something other than population. He went so far as to add a rider to President Johnson's signature foreign aid authorization bill, which would stay implementation of the Supreme Court's ruling until January 1, 1965. He said this would give time to amend the constitution. Ultimately, the rider was defeated.

Several state legislatures were watching these Supreme Court cases, and the arguments made by Senator Dirksen and came to the conclusion that they also disagreed with the court. There being no other remedy for this disagreement, they looked to Article V of the Constitution. In 1963, Arkansas, Idaho, Kansas, Missouri, Montana, Nevada, Oklahoma, South Carolina, South Dakota, Texas, Washington, and Wyoming all filed applications for an Article V convention to prohibit the federal government from entering into state redistricting. Most of these applications suggested the following language for an amendment (*109 Cong. Rec. 2769, 2281, 2769, 5968, 3854, 9942, 1172-73, 10441-42, 14639, 5867, 4779, 1963*):

SECTION 1. No provision of this Constitution, or any amendment thereto, shall restrict or limit any State in the apportionment of representation in its legislature.

SEC. 2. The Judicial power of the United States shall not extend to any suit in law or equity, or to any controversy relating to apportionment of representation in a State legislature.

SEC. 3. This article shall be inoperative unless it shall have been ratified as an amendment to the Constitution by the legislatures of three-fourth of the several States within 7 years from the date of its submission.

These states clearly saw the apportionment of their own legislatures as a state sovereignty item, and not one of federal supremacy. In 1963, Virginia joined with their application. Then in 1965, Alabama, Arizona, Georgia, Kentucky, Louisiana, Maryland, Minnesota, Mississippi, Missouri, Nebraska, New Hampshire, North Carolina, Tennessee, Utah, Florida, and New Mexico joined with their applications bringing the total to 28 states. Only 6 more were needed to reach the two-thirds threshold of 34.

Also in 1965, Congress passed the Voting Rights Act of 1965. Among its many provisions were some redistricting restrictions. Section 5 said that voting jurisdictions in a "covered area" were required to submit any changes in voting laws, including redistricting, to the Department of Justice or a three-judge panel from the federal district court of the District of Columbia for "pre clearance" prior to implementation. A formula was set out in Section 4(b) to determine which jurisdictions are subject to preclearance.

In 1967, Colorado, Illinois, Indiana, and North Dakota submitted their applications making the total 32. Two years went by before Iowa sent in their application in 1969 making it 33, only one state short.

What happened in Wisconsin may well have had a detrimental effect in the attempts to reclaim state sovereignty that would last for the next 50 years. In 1969, Assemblyman Kenneth Merkel, a Republican from Brookfield, Wisconsin and a leading member of the Wisconsin John Birch Society, reintroduced a measure to make an application for a convention to propose an amendment to the U.S. Constitution. The resolution had passed in the Senate in 1967 but died in the House in the rush to adjourn. He referred to the amendment as the "Dirksen Amendment" in honor of Illinois Senator Everett Dirksen, who had died on September 7th. His resolution was defeated when all 47 Democrats were joined by 14 Republicans to vote it down in the 100 member House. Had this measure passed and been transmitted to Congress, Congress would have been obligated to call an Article V convention to propose amendments.

No other state has ever submitted an application for this amendment. But what if Wisconsin had become the 34th state? With 34 states so united in purpose, would that have forced a convention, an amendment, and presumably gotten an additional four states for ratification. What would have been the effect over the last fifty years? If in 1970, the states would have drawn a line on federal overreach and established a workable mode to keep and regain state sovereignty in many areas, our country would be so much different now. But more on this in the conclusion.

Consequently, federal control over states redistricting was in force, and under the rules in Section 4(b), jurisdictions were added to the coverage area requiring preclearance. The coverage formula and preclearance parts were supposed to expire in five years. However, Congress reauthorized these parts, and in 2006 reauthorized them for an additional 25 years. The test in section 4(b), established in 1965, and reauthorized in 2006, which placed a jurisdiction in the coverage area, and then required preclearance, still turned on the review of circumstances in the 1960s and early 1970s, 40 years ago.

In 2011, Shelby County, Alabama sued the U.S. Attorney General, Eric Holder in the District Court of the District of Columbia on the grounds that Section 4(b) and Section 5 were unconstitutional on their face. The court upheld the provisions, and the Appeals court affirmed that decision. However, in 2013, the Supreme Court, in a 5 to 4 decision, held Section 4(b) unconstitutional but left Section 5 in place. By 2013 jurisdictions in the "covered area" included all of Alabama, Alaska, Arizona, Georgia, Louisiana, Mississippi, South Carolina, Texas, and Virginia. It also included three counties in California, five counties in Florida, three counties in New York, forty counties in North Carolina, two counties in South Dakota, and two townships in Michigan. Since the formula to determine coverage in section 4(b) was no longer law, no jurisdictions could remain in the "covered area" and consequently no longer had to obtain preclearance for changes in voting laws or redistricting.

In review, because of a clear attempt to remove black voters from the city limits of Tuskegee, Alabama, the federal government over reacted. In this overreaction, the congress in the Voting Rights Act of 1965 took control of state redistricting which is clearly the role of state governments. The Supreme Court was complicit time and again in upholding this over-reach for over 50 years. Initially, 33 states sought to protect their sovereignty in this area via the use of Article V and a constitutional amendment to clarify the limit of federal power. Any one of the other 17 states could have tipped the balance, but did not. The consequence was 50 years of federal oppression for the jurisdictions in the "covered area". Perhaps Justice Scalia is right, amending the Constitution should be hard but not that hard.

Since 1970, twenty states have rescinded their applications for the purpose of proposing an apportionment amendment, leaving the active applications at thirteen states. They are Alabama, Arkansas, Florida, Illinois, Indiana, Iowa, Kentucky, Minnesota, Mississippi, Missouri, Nebraska, North Carolina, and Washington.

In Baker, the court said trees and acres do not get representation. Remember in the Direct Election of Senators we spoke about need and issues beyond population? Here it is again. The founding fathers saw it necessary to provide for the representation of States in the U.S. Senate independent of the people residing in those states. Discrimination aside for just a moment, why would that not apply in a state just as well as in the nation? At least one chamber should be able to represent those issues which transcend the wants and desires of the population. The question is how to establish what those needs and issues are, and how to assign one chamber to protect them.

If you want to avoid fifty years of unconstitutional interference by the federal government, pressure your state legislator to unleash the power of Article V.

Below is a graph showing the number of states with new applications, rescissions, and active applications by year:

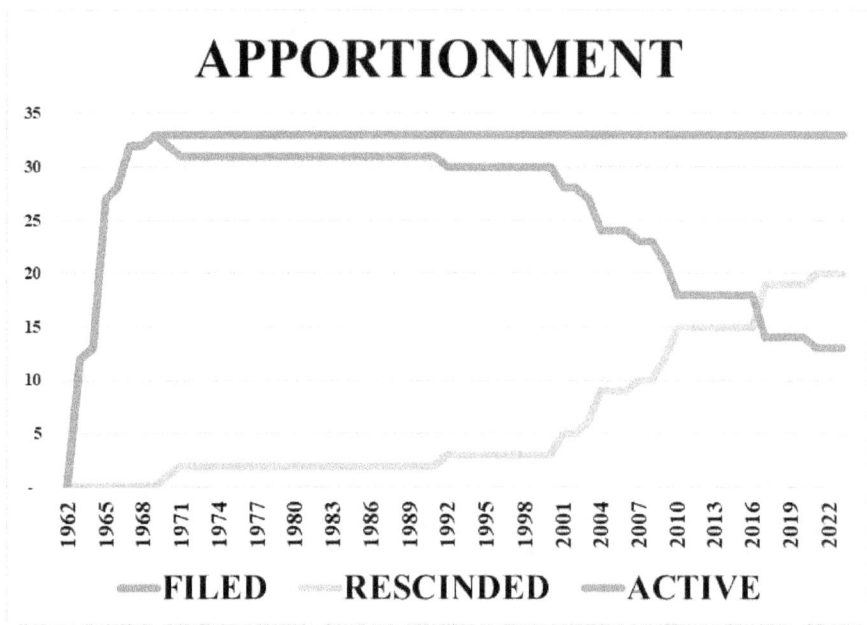

APPORTIONMENT

REVENUE SHARING

A father says to his five children, "Since you are working now, I'm going to take half of your earnings to provide for things you can't do yourself. If, at the end of the month, I have some left, I'll give that to your mother to offset the cost of the things she does for you." If these children are between the ages of seven and fifteen, this is a workable process, and an exercise in responsible spending. On the other hand, if these children are between thirty and forty, this is highly unworkable. If the father is the federal government, and the mother is the state governments, and the children are the citizens, this is insane. However, that, in a nutshell, is the theory of revenue sharing pushed by many politicians and economists in the 1960s.

John Maynard Keynes was a British economist who lived from 1883 to 1946. He was an early advocate for a government role in setting fiscal and monetary policies to manage the economy. He believed that this would mitigate the effects of recessions and depressions. Most capitalist governments had adopted his theories by the end of World War II. A key part of his theories included the concept that governments should engage in deficit spending during recessions. Franklin Roosevelt adopted this policy during the depression, and kept up the deficit spending through the end of World War II.

Milton Friedman was an American economist who lived from 1912 to 2006. During the 1960s, he became the anti-Keynesian in economic discourse, in particular when it came to government policies. He was most influential in the 1980s with Ronald Reagan and Margaret Thatcher. His views indicated that deficit spending would result in inflation and stagnant economic growth, called stagflation. While many still hang on to Keynesian philosophy, most believe that Friedman wins the argument.

Walter Heller was an American economist who lived from 1915 to 1987. He was most influential in the 1960s as an advisor to John F. Kennedy as chairman of the Council of Economic Advisors from 1961 to 1964. He was a devotee of Keynes, and therefore, a critic of Friedman. He has been noted as saying *"Some of them are Friedmanly, some Friedmanian, some Friedmanesque, some Friedmanic and some*

Friedmaniacs. ' I suppose I should confess to being a Friedmaniac, and not a Keynesian.

(Memorandum to William Carmichael as quoted on page 206 of Valdes, Pinochet's Economists.)

Heller gave a speech on June 6, 1960, in which he suggested that an agreed share of federal income tax revenue should be diverted to the states. Since the FDR administration, the federal government had funded lots of activities in the states. That funding had come with very specific instructions and limits on how the money could be spent. What was different about the Heller proposal was that this agreed percentage of federal income tax would be diverted to state use with very few if any strings attached as to how it could be used. In Heller's mind, this would be necessary as the growing economy returned to federal surpluses. The concept of a federal surplus sounds like a pipe dream to most of us today. But in Heller's defense, in the 14 years from 1947 to 1960, the federal government had a surplus in 6 of them, a deficit in 6 of them, and 1960 had neither. The total of all the deficits and surpluses for that 14-year period was a $1 billion deficit.

There is an excellent research paper on how the federal government met with the Heller plan, and it can be found here:

Worsnop, R. L. (1964). Federal-state revenue sharing. Editorial research reports 1964 *(Vol. II).*
http://library.cqpress.com/cqresearcher/cqresrre1964122300

The more relevant question to us in this book is how did the states react to the concept? First, a key aspect to the Heller plan was the assertion that there were not sufficient taxing opportunities available since the income tax had been implemented. State legislators are, after all, politicians and recognized an opportunity to take credit for implementing new state benefits and services, or lowering state taxes while not being seen as responsible for the taxes which enabled those programs. They could spend the "federal money" while at the same time commiserating with the taxpayers on the evil federal taxes. However, by 1965, the federal government did not appear to be moving in the direction of any revenue sharing which did not include strings.

Illinois and Ohio were the first to submit applications for an Article V convention to propose an amendment requiring revenue sharing by the federal government. Alabama, Georgia, and Texas joined in 1967 and Florida and New Hampshire in 1969 and New Jersey in 1970. Then the word was out and the flood gates opened with eight more states joining the call in 1971. These were Delaware, Louisiana, Massachusetts, North Dakota, Oregon, Rhode Island, South Dakota, and West Virginia. Iowa was the last to join in 1972. This brought the total number of states making the call to 19, well short of the 34-state threshold.

In October of 1972, Congress passed the State and Local Fiscal Assistance Act (General Revenue Sharing), and President Nixon signed it into law. This was not completely without strings attached, but what it did was to consolidate about 100 specific categories of federal grants into 6 general categories. The allocation of $30 billion was to be distributed in seven lumps between 1972 and 1976 and would cover Urban community development, rural community development, manpower training, law enforcement, transportation, and education.

The program was due to expire in 1976, but President Ford declared it a resounding success and threw his support behind measures to reauthorize it. Congress did reauthorize it in 1976. It was reauthorized for a second time under President Carter in 1980 but only for local jurisdictions, meaning specific city and county but not state-wide programs.

In 1983, it was reauthorized for the last time by President Reagan, but with severe cuts in the amounts. Remember, Milton Friedman was now the key economic advisor, and Keynesian philosophies were being phased out.

It can be noted here that Calvin Coolidge was Ronald Reagan's favorite President. About taxes, Coolidge was quoted as saying "Collecting more taxes than absolutely necessary is legalized robbery." The Coolidge administration was actually the architect of "Reaganomics", which called for lower tax rates in order to increase tax revenue dollars. The plan worked in the 1920s under Coolidge and also in the 1980s under Reagan.

However, increased federal revenues do not reduce the deficits when the spending grows faster than the revenue. We should recall that the Heller plan was predicated on a return to federal surpluses. After all, half of the previous 14 years had seen a federal surplus. But that was history from a 1960 view. History from a 1986 view was quite different. In the 26 years from 1961 to 1986, only one year had a surplus of $3 billion. All of the other 25 had deficits, and the total deficit for the 26-year period was $1,515 billion. The 1986 deficit alone was $221 billion. The Reagan tax cuts in the late 80s lowered the deficits by $75 billion, but spending remained out of control. In fact, there would not be a federal surplus until 1998 when the full effects of the 1994 "Contract with America" took hold. From 1998 to 2001, the federal government had a surplus each of those four years totaling $559 billion.

This effort for an Article V convention was very short lived and reached just 19 states making applications. All of those applications remained in force through the end of the 20th century, but eight have been rescinded in the 21st century as part of many states' efforts to clean up their open applications.

In order to avoid dad managing your money and giving the leftovers to mom, pressure your state legislator to unleash Article V.

The graph below shows the number states with new, rescinded and active applications by year:

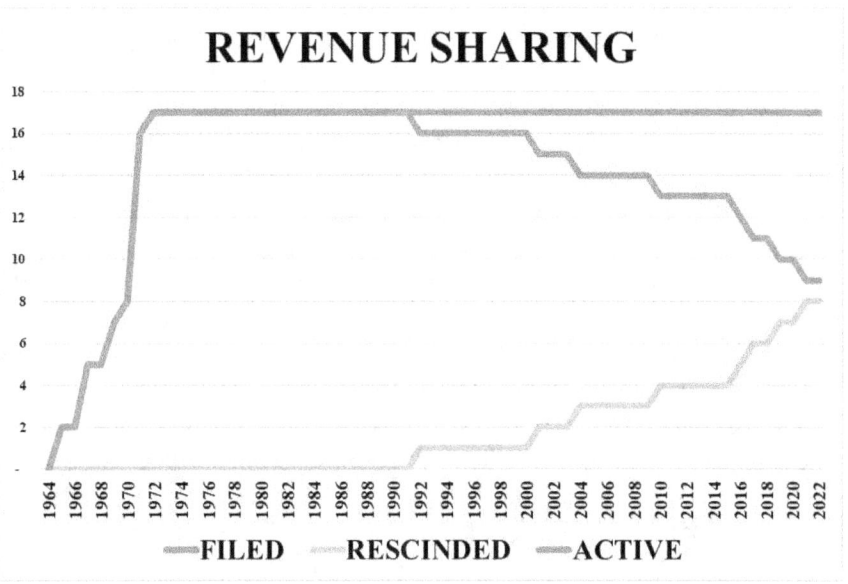

RIGHT TO LIFE

Almost everyone would agree that the fundamental purpose of government is to protect the lives, liberties and properties of its citizens. Liberty surely implies the right to decide for ones-self what actions or methods are appropriate in their own circumstances. Most of us would also agree that one person's liberty does not extend to infringements upon another person's liberty. For this reason, our government makes laws to help distinguish which person has the greater right to their liberty, and therefore, when the other must live with an infringement. The courts then have the duty to decide when or if a law has been broken, or which person in a controversy should prevail.

Our Constitution shares the power of law making between the federal and state legislatures. In the specific areas where the power is given to the federal government, those federal laws are superior to any state law which is in conflict with it. Our bill of rights, the first ten amendments to the Constitution, prohibits federal laws and procedures which intrude on certain specified rights. Further, the ninth amendment provides that people have other rights not specifically called out in the first eight amendments. The fourteenth amendment has been interpreted to extend the federal bill of rights to protect citizens from state laws as well and also gives the federal government the power to enforce that protection.

Anthony Comstock was born in Connecticut in 1844. He served in the 17th Connecticut Infantry during the Civil War. He was appointed as a special agent of the U.S. Postal Service in 1873, and served in that capacity until 1907. During his service in the Civil War, he was appalled by the profanity and debauchery of the Union soldiers. Comstock decided his calling was to be the "weeder in God's Garden", and began to use his position as Postal Inspector to eliminate pornography from the mail, and as a result of his influence, Congress passed the Comstock Act in 1873. The Comstock Act prohibited sending "obscene, lewd or lascivious" items through the mail. Because he was a Postal Inspector, he became the "enforcer", so to speak, of the new law. The law specifically listed contraceptives as obscene materials.

Contraception has been sought after at least since the time of Genesis when Onan made every effort not to impregnate his dead brother's wife. Aristotle proposed various oils to be used as spermicides, and a Roman writer of Natural History counseled abstinence. Casanova (1725-1798) experimented with many forms of birth control including the rind of half a lemon as a primitive diaphragm. In 1827 scientists discovered the female egg, and in 1843 that conception occurs when the sperm enters the egg. In 1839, Charles Goodyear invented vulcanized rubber and used it to make condoms, intrauterine devices and diaphragms. By 1873 there were a large variety of birth control products available from catalogs, pharmacists, dry-goods stores and even rubber vendors. Given this history, the Comstock Act was not well received by those that were purchasing these products on a regular basis.

In 1883, Francis Galton, Charles Darwin's cousin, published a book titled "Inquiries into Human Fertility and Its Development". In this book, he coined and defined the term "eugenics" which gave birth to an entire movement. The Eugenics movement was centered around the concept that the human race could be perfected by essentially managing which parents may produce children. German biologist Alfred Ploetz picked up on the concept and ultimately had a huge influence on Nazi race-based eugenics.

In 1890, Emil Knauer discovered chemicals that control the body's metabolic processes. In 1905 after many years studying these chemical substances, they were named hormones, meaning to "incite" in Greek.

Margaret Sanger, was born in 1879, the sixth child of a poor family in Corning, New York. By 1912 she had become a nurse on New York City's lower east side. She was looking for a "magic pill" to be used as a contraceptive. In 1914, she published a journal in which she advised and instructed women to avoid pregnancy when sick or poor. The New York City postmaster banned the journal under the Comstock Law. That June, Sanger used the term "birth control" in an issue of The Woman Rebel, and in August she was indicted on nine counts under the Comstock Law. She fled to England to continue her work. She returned to New York in 1916 to face trial, but the charges were dropped. Without fear, she began a new publication, Birth Control Review. Sanger and her sister along with a friend opened the first birth control clinic in Brooklyn. Ten days later, the vice squad raided the clinic, arrested all three women and confiscated the entire inventory of contraceptive devices.

The raid, arrests, and confiscation were done under the New York anti-obscenity law which supplemented the Comstock Law. Section 1142 made it illegal to distribute, advertise or sell contraception materials as well as restricting the discussion of this information. However, Section 1145 made physicians exempt from 1142. Sanger made bail the next morning, and on November 14th, reopened her clinic. The women were arrested again two days later. The court tried the women separately, all were found guilty of different charges and received different sentences. Sanger got 30 days in the Queens County Penitentiary. After her release in March of 1916, Sanger filed an appeal, which she lost because she was not a physician. However, the ruling seemed to broaden the rights of physicians to prescribe contraceptives if a married woman should avoid pregnancy for general health reasons. People v. Sanger was later cited in federal court cases and in 1936 resulted in allowing physicians to distribute contraceptives through the U.S. Postal Service.

By 1906, the German eugenics movement had crossed the Atlantic. The American Breeder's Association was established to study and promote genetics as well as plant and animal breeding research. At the request of Charles Davenport, a Harvard biologist, the American Breeder's Association set up a Committee on Eugenics. In 1907, Indiana passed the first sterilization law to prevent pregnancies of "idiots" or "imbeciles" as well as certain classes of criminals. By the end of World War I, there were eugenics organizations throughout the western hemisphere. The American Eugenics Society was established in 1926 with over 1,200 members including Margret Sanger.

In 1921 Margaret Sanger established the American Birth Control League and in 1923 established the first legal birth control clinic in conjunction with Dr. Dorothy Bocker, a licensed physician.

Meanwhile, science continued its march of discovery and learning. In 1926, scientists discovered that the pituitary gland is the control center for human reproduction, and the first pregnancy test was created. In 1928 the critical role of the hormone progesterone in starting and sustaining pregnancy was discovered. Estrogen was isolated in 1929. In 1941 Russell Marker found a way to make synthetic progesterone from wild yams. In 1945 Fuller Albright produced a report on serious menstrual disorder and postulated that preventing ovulation would be a way to treat it, as well as becoming a method of birth control. He called it hormone therapy.

Katharine Dexter McCormick was born in 1875 to a wealthy and prominent family in Dexter, Michigan. In 1904 she became the first woman to graduate from the Massachusetts Institute of Technology with a science degree. She married Stanley McCormick, the heir to the International Harvester fortune. In 1906, Stanley was diagnosed with schizophrenia, and fearing it was hereditary, Katharine became determined not to have any children. Katharine McCormick and Margaret Sanger met in 1917 at one of Sanger's lectures and formed a lifelong friendship. In 1947, Stanley McCormick died and left the entire family fortune in Katharine's control. In 1950, at age 75, she determined to use her fortune to fund birth control research projects, and contacted Sanger to guide her in placing research grants.

In August of 1930, the world assembly of Anglican bishops met and passed a resolution making limited acceptance of birth control, which was adopted by the majority of Protestant Churches. In December of that same year, Pope Pius XI issued an encyclical, calling birth control by any means a sin. The Vatican accepted the choice of not having sex during ovulation, the rhythm method. These two opposing views set up a split view in the country, and a fracture in the Comstock Law. Contraception was no longer a clear moral imperative.

By 1951, Margaret Sanger's organization had become The Planned Parenthood Federation of America and ran 200 birth control clinics. At age 72, she was still looking for someone who could create a magic pill for contraception. She was introduced to Gregory Pincus at a dinner party and asked him about the possibility. He told her that it might be possible with hormone therapy but would require significant funding. She managed to get a small grant from Planned Parenthood to allow him to begin the research. Neither Sanger or Pincus were aware that Carl Djerassi in a small lab in Mexico City had created an effective oral form of synthetic progesterone. Djerassi nor his company had any interest in its use as a contraceptive. In January of 1952, Pincus had proven progesterone effective in preventing ovulation in rabbits and rats, but was out of money. Planned Parenthood decided the work was too risky and his project stagnated for lack of funds.

John Rock and his twin sister Eleanor were born in Marlborough, Massachusetts in 1890 to a working class Irish Catholic family. By 1924 he was an assistant in obstetrics at Harvard Medical School focused on treating women with fertility problems. By the 1940s, Rock was teaching medical students about birth control, covertly of course. He put his reputation on the line in 1943 and publicly asked the state to allow physicians to advise patients on birth control. In 1949, still a devout Catholic and despite the Pope's pronouncement, he co-authored a book on Voluntary Parenthood. This was targeted at explaining birth control methods to an audience tired of coping with unwanted pregnancies.

Meanwhile, the chief chemist at G.D. Searle, Frank Colton, had also developed an oral form of synthetic progesterone in 1952. That same year Gregory Pincus attended a scientific conference where he met John Rock. Pincus was surprised to learn of Rock already testing chemical contraceptives on women. In 1953, Sanger realized that McCormick could fund Pincus's research and arranged a meeting where Pincus walked away with a $40,000 check and a promise of more when needed. At this point Pincus had the money to proceed, and the knowledge that Rock already had something that would work. He realized that a magic pill would require FDA approval, and that would hinge on human trials. He enlisted Rock to test the drug on his female patients, but with the restrictive laws of Massachusetts, they called it a fertility study. The pills for the test were provided by Searle. In 1955 with conclusive results that none of the 50 women in the study had ovulated, Pincus announced the results at the International Planned Parenthood League conference in Tokyo, and Rock presented a paper stating that the progesterone pill inhibits ovulation. Now the whole scientific world knew there was a birth control pill.

In 1959, the FDA approved the pill, Enovid for therapeutic use for severe menstrual disorders. By the end of the year, a massive number of women had been diagnosed with menstrual disorders, presumably for a prescription for the pill and the contraceptive purpose. Searle, of course, could see the dollar signs and applied to the FDA to use the same pill for contraceptive purposes. The application was based on a trial with 897 women. Searle received the approval of the 10mg dose in 1960, and in a cost saving move applied for approval of 2.5mg and 5mg doses. As soon as the field trials were completed, they received the approval.

In 1961, Connecticut law still made it a crime to use birth control. In defiance of that law, Dr. Buxton and Estelle Griswold opened four Planned Parenthood clinics. Griswold was the executive director of Planned Parenthood in Connecticut. They were arrested and charged under the Connecticut Law, and the Comstock Act. They took the case all the way to the Supreme Court where they won a 7 to 2 decision. The decision, in 1965, created the right to privacy in case law. Justice William O. Douglas wrote, *"Would we allow the police to search the sacred precincts of marital bedrooms for telltale signs of the use of contraceptives? The very idea is repulsive to the notions of privacy surrounding the marriage relationship." (U.S. Supreme Court: Griswold v. Connecticut, 381 U.S. 479 (1965).* The court held that the "right to privacy" was implied by the specific provisions in the First, Third, Fourth and Fifth Amendments.

In 1972, Eisenstadt v Baird extended the holdings in Griswold to unmarried couples. In this finding, the court said that to protect the right to privacy of a married couple but not an unmarried couple violated the Equal Protection Clause of the Fourteenth Amendment.

Norma Nelson was born in Louisiana in 1947 and the family later moved to Houston. Norma began having trouble with the law at age 10 when she robbed a gas station and ran away to Oklahoma City. Through the courts, she ended up as a resident of the State School for Girls in Gainesville, Texas, where she lived on and off from age 11 to 15. When not at the State School, she lived at home in Houston. Her father left the family when she was 13, and she was then raised by her violent alcoholic mother. She met and married Woody McCorvey in 1963 at age 16. By 1965, Woody had become abusive and Norma left him, moved in with her mother, and gave birth to her first child. She developed a drug and alcohol problem and ultimately the child was released for adoption and her mother kicked her out of the house. Norma became pregnant again the next year and released that child for adoption as well. In 1969 she became pregnant a third time and moved to Dallas. She decided she did not want to have another baby and began looking for an abortion, which was not legal in Texas except to protect the life of the mother. Norma ultimately met attorneys Linda Coffee and Sarah Weddington, who were looking for a test case to challenge abortion laws. They filed suit naming Dallas district attorney Henry Wade. No one could know how high a profile the case would become, but Henry Wade was no stranger to the legal spotlight. He had prosecuted Jack Ruby for the death of Lee Harvey Oswald in 1964. By the time Norma's case worked its way through the courts, Norma had the baby and released it for adoption, and for court purposes had become Jane Roe.

The Texas district court ruled that the abortion law was unconstitutional because it violated Jane's right to privacy. The case was appealed and finally arrived at the Supreme Court. On January 22, 1973 the Supreme Court ruled, 7 to 2, that the Texas abortion law was unconstitutional on the basis of the right to privacy. The right to privacy was established as a fundamental right in Griswold v. Connecticut in 1965, which had made laws banning contraception illegal. Now, Roe v. Wade has made abortion legal.

In his dissent, Justice Byron White wrote (*U.S. Supreme Court: Roe v. Wade 410 U.S. 113, 1973*):

I find nothing in the language or history of the Constitution to support the Court's judgment. The Court simply fashions and announces a new constitutional right for pregnant women and, with scarcely any reason or authority for its action, invests that right with sufficient substance to override most existing state abortion statutes. The upshot is that the people and the legislatures of the 50 States are constitutionally disentitled to weigh the relative importance of the continued existence and development of the fetus, on the one hand, against a spectrum of possible impacts on the woman, on the other hand. As an exercise of raw judicial power, the Court perhaps has authority to do what it does today; but, in my view, its judgment is an improvident and extravagant exercise of the power of judicial review that the Constitution extends to this Court.

Justice William Rehnquist dissented with this (*U.S. Supreme Court: Roe v. Wade 410 U.S. 113, 1973*):

To reach its result, the Court necessarily has had to find within the scope of the Fourteenth Amendment a right that was apparently completely unknown to the drafters of the Amendment. As early as 1821, the first state law dealing directly with abortion was enacted by the Connecticut Legislature. By the time of the adoption of the Fourteenth Amendment in 1868, there were at least 36 laws enacted by state or territorial legislatures limiting abortion. While many States have amended or updated their laws, 21 of the laws on the books in 1868 remain in effect today.

My question goes further than either dissent. I think we all have a right to be left alone by our government, which can be construed as privacy. Remember the government should protect the life, liberty and property of its citizens. My right to be left alone, does not however extend to allowing me to harm the life, liberty or property of another, just because we are "in private". The government is obliged to violate my privacy both to prevent, or prosecute me when I do, violate someone else's rights. This, then, begs the question of whether a fetus is a person deserving of the protection of the law and when does a fetus achieve that status? Finally, in the Unborn Victims of Violence Act of 2004, the law defined a "child in utero" as a member of the species Homo sapiens, at any stage of development, who is carried in the womb. However, the law only affords this unborn person protection if they are injured or killed during the commission of listed federal crimes of violence. Why is this child in utero protected from the violence of some, but not the violence of its mother or doctor? Perhaps this is at least a positive step on the path of recovery from our legal schizophrenia when it comes to protection of the unborn. Proponents of abortion claim the "right to choose" on behalf of the mother. Given the history of contraception science and the plethora of contraceptive options available in 1973, and more so in 2023, the choice should have been made prior to pregnancy. After pregnancy, the mother still has two choices, one to raise the child or the other to release that child for adoption.

At the time of the Roe decision, only 1 state, Pennsylvania, had a law against abortion with no exceptions at all. There were 29 states with a single exception, to protect the life of the mother. In Mississippi, there was an exception for rape. Alabama and Massachusetts had exceptions for the health of the mother, and 13 states had exceptions for the health of the mother, rape, incest or likely damaged fetus. The remaining 4 states allowed abortion at a doctor's discretion.

Indiana was first, in 1973 to make an application for an Article V convention to propose an amendment to reserve the power of deciding on the legality of abortion to the states, and remove it from the power of the federal government.

In 1975 Missouri submitted an application which contained this language in its proposed amendment (*121 Cong. Rec. 12,867, 1975*):

"Section 1. With respect to the right of life, the word person as used in this article and in the Fifth and Fourteenth Articles of Amendment to the Constitution of the United States applies to all human beings irrespective of age, health, function or condition of dependency, including their unborn offspring at every stage of their biological development.

"Sec. 2. No unborn person shall be deprived of life by any person; provided, however, that nothing in this article shall prohibit a law permitting only those medical procedures required to prevent the death of the mother.

"Sec. 3. The Congress and the several states-have-power to enforce this article by appropriate legislation.

In 1976, the Speaker of the House presented a memorial of Louisiana's application. In 1977 through 1980, an additional 16 states submitted applications with essentially the same language as Missouri. From 1980 through 1991, no further action was taken relative to proposing amendments to protect the right to life.

Many cases have been heard in the interim which altered the reach of Roe v. Wade and allowed for some limitations which states could place on abortions. Between 1992 and 2022, 9 states have rescinded their applications for a right to life amendment leaving 10 with active applications. In 2022, the Supreme Court finally overturned Roe v. Wade effectively removing federal action limiting what restrictions states could place on abortion. Most states have responded to this with some legislation, some placing sweeping restrictions on abortions and others creating state laws to allow virtually all abortions.

Maybe, someday, Americans will be able to fully abandon this legal schizophrenia and realize that the time for choice is prior to conception. That choice is made possible through all of the contraceptive options our incredible scientific advances have provided us. When contraception fails us, or we fail to partake of any, and a child is created, there are still two remaining choices. That mother can love that child by cherishing it and raising it or releasing it to be adopted by a loving couple who can't conceive their own. As a father to three adopted children, I can attest that there is no greater gift that can be received than that of a child.

Perhaps we have found something beyond a voting population which requires representation?

Permanently remove the settlement of this argument from the federal government and put it back in the state where it belongs. More permanently, insist that your state government protect the life of the most vulnerable, the unborn. Pressure your state legislator to unleash the power of Article V.

Below is a graph showing the number of states with new applications, rescissions, and active applications by year:

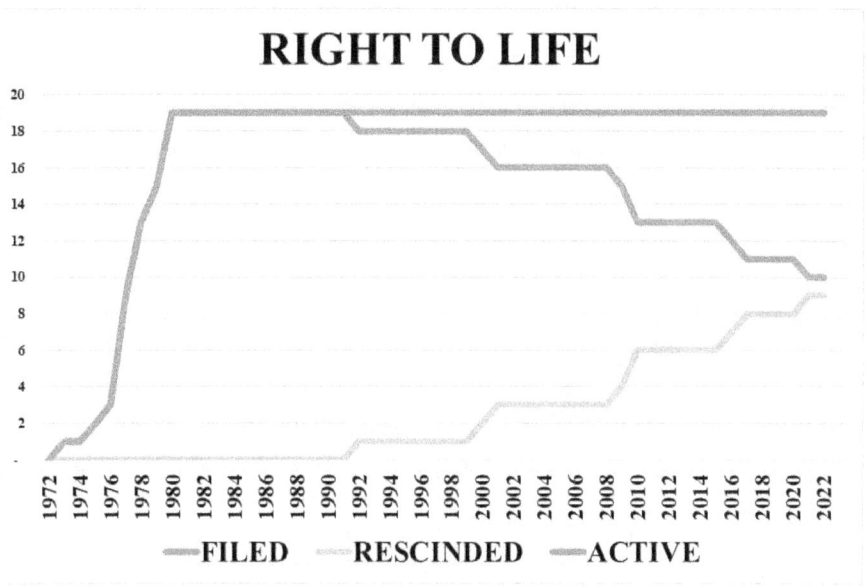

CONVENTION OF STATES PROJECT

Over the last 130 years, or so, our federal government has vastly broadened the areas it has jurisdiction over, and the power it has in those jurisdictions. It has behaved as though there is no limit on the money it can spend, the debt it can create and the taxes it can implement. Those elected to office in Washington, the President, Vice President, 435 members of the House of Representatives, and the 100 members of the Senate, either cannot, or will not, check the growth of that government. Those that get elected and discover that they cannot fix Washington give up and go home. Those that will not fix Washington continue to be reelected, and they use two tactics to do so. Some point fingers at the problem and draw connecting lines between the growth of the problem and the politicians on the other side of the aisle. Others promise to shift the spending so that their constituents will receive a bigger and bigger piece of the hand out pie. The results of coming up with more and more handouts creates more and more agencies and produces more and more spending, higher and higher taxes and higher and higher debt.

During the entire time that this has been happening, an enterprising few have objected to the creation of new benefits, new agencies and new areas of federal control. They have repeatedly challenged the constitutional authority of new agencies to exist, new benefits to be created and the coercion pushed on state and local governments to join in the expansion. Many of them have found their way to the Supreme Court, as though that were the one branch of the federal government which would stop it. But seriously, those justices were mostly educated and came of age in a system of jurisprudence which is built on an inability to recognize, much less correct its errors in thought. The federal court system, like the halls of Congress and the White House, has had its dissenters. Sometimes those dissents have, in a few decades, been vindicated with a rare overturning of a major decision which puts us back on the right path.

We have looked at the response of state legislatures to this ever-growing federal power, broadening federal jurisdiction, higher spending, growing debt, and extensive longevity in office of elected and appointed officials. Every state legislature, except Hawaii, has submitted at least one application for an article V convention to propose amendments in response to, and to correct some federal action or inaction. In most of these cases, state legislators have been the main proponents and sponsors of these actions.

Something new occurred in the 2008 – 2012 presidential election cycle. This was the popular "grassroots" rise of a thing called the Tea Party Movement. On February 19, 2009, CNBC reporter Rick Santelli, speaking from the floor of the Chicago Mercantile Exchange, called for a tea party. The reference was to the Boston Tea Party, a popular movement to protest the tea tax and delivery of tea to the colonies. This elicited a response the next day by the Nationwide Tea Party Coalition. The very next day, about 50 conservative activists held a conference call, and the Tea Party Movement was born.

On that conference call were people like Amy Kremer, an ex-flight attendant turned political activist. She was involved in organizing Tea Party protests in 2009. She said she was "just a mom who was sick and fed up with what was going on in Washington". She was a co-founder of the Tea Party Patriots, but left soon after to join a different group, the Tea Party Express. There, she worked to garner support for many of the "Tea Party Candidates". She remains an activist and shows up all over the country.

Another person on that call was Jenny Beth Martin. She was also a co-founder of Tea Party Patriots and became a highly paid leader of the non-profit. Martin also was co-founder of the Tea Party Patriots Citizens Fund, a PAC established to counter Carl Rove's Conservative Victory Project.

A third co-founder of the Tea Party Patriots was Mark Meckler. He and his wife had a coffee house in Nevada City, California, which they sold in 1997 and then started a company making snow skiing equipment. Being an attorney, he eventually established his own law practice focused on internet advertising law. He attended a Tea Party protest in Sacramento in February, 2009 where he caught the Tea Party fever. He and Martin co-authored a book, *Tea Party Patriots: The Second American Revolution*. He became critical of the Tea Party Express being too close to the Republican Party, and when the Tea Party Patriots sponsored the Southern Republican Leadership Conference, he split with that organization.

The movement had a dramatic impact on the internal workings of the Republican Party both on ideology and candidate selection for the next several national elections. Tea Party chapters, over 2,000, were formed all across the country. Those participating in the protests, political campaigns, and other activities had high hopes of changing the direction of the federal government. The 2010 midterm election was crowded with Tea Party supported candidates. With 129 for the House, and 9 for the Senate, NBC said that 32% of the candidates were either backed by, or were themselves, Tea Party members. This set up a confrontation between the "establishment" incumbent Republicans and the "grassroots" Tea Party Republicans in the 2010 primaries. Many of them won the primaries and set up great expectations for the general election in November. Many of those hopes were dashed when Tea Party primary successes were defeated by their Democrat opponents in November.

In the end, 2010 added a few Tea Party candidates to congress and 2012 added a few more. By the 2016 elections, however, these hopes had faded with the realization that a majority could not be created or, for that matter, a very effective minority. While the Tea Party people and many more individuals continue to be a conservative thorn in the side of the Republican Party establishment, the movement, as the Tea Party, has largely stalled.

Shortly after Meckler left the Tea Party Patriots, noting that it was too much aligned with the Republican Party, and that a large number of its members were not Republicans. Meckler then founded another organization, Citizens for Self-Governance to focus on broadening the philosophical reach of the idea of self-governance outside of the Tea Party movement. Many (if not most) of the Tea Party chapters' applications for non-profit status with the IRS were being slow-walked, if not outright stalled by the agency. Through his organization, Meckler helped file a class action lawsuit against the IRS for targeting conservative organizations. As a result, the Supreme Court issued a unanimous rebuke to the IRS. Also, as a project of this organization, Meckler established Convention of States Action. This project was focused on the concept of a popular movement to champion state legislators to push for an Article V convention to propose amendments that would rein in the federal overreach.

This is where something truly new and different is being done with the use of the Article V application. The Convention of States Project starts with the concept of self-governance. That is to say that each American has a responsibility to participate in the governing process. This extends far beyond voting in elections, far beyond doing due diligence on candidates before voting in elections, but extends into active advocacy for the policies and laws we intend our candidates to champion. Accordingly, the Convention of States Project has established a nationwide, all volunteer organization for the advocacy of using an Article V convention to curtail the federal government's overreach.

Early on in the process, the project enlisted the help of constitutional lawyers such as co-founder, Michael Ferris. Ferris has successfully argued over 40 Supreme Court cases. Together, they developed model legislation for state legislatures to use in an Article V application with the object of limiting the federal government but not specifying amendment language to be used.

That model resolution reads as follows (Convention of States Action, n.d):

Whereas, the Founders of our Constitution empowered State Legislators to be guardians of liberty against future abuses of power by the federal government, and

Whereas, the federal government has created a crushing national debt through improper and imprudent spending, and

Whereas, the federal government has invaded the legitimate roles of the states through the manipulative process of federal mandates, most of which are unfunded to a great extent, and

Whereas, the federal government has ceased to live under a proper interpretation of the Constitution of the United States, and

Whereas, it is the solemn duty of the States to protect the liberty of our people—particularly for the generations to come—by proposing Amendments to the Constitution of the United States through a

Convention of the States under Article V for the purpose of restraining these and related abuses of power,

Be it therefore resolved by the legislature of the State of __:

Section 1. The legislature of the State of __ hereby applies to Congress, under the provisions of Article V of the Constitution of the United States, for the calling of a convention of the states limited to proposing amendments to the Constitution of the United States that impose fiscal restraints on the federal government, limit the power and jurisdiction of the federal government, and limit the terms of office for its officials and for members of Congress.

Section 2. The secretary of state is hereby directed to transmit copies of this application to the President and Secretary of the United States Senate and to the Speaker and Clerk of the United States House of Representatives, and copies to the members of the said Senate and House of Representatives from this State; also, to transmit copies hereof to the presiding officers of each of the legislative houses in the several States, requesting their cooperation.

Section 3. This application constitutes a continuing application in accordance with Article V of the Constitution of the United States until the legislatures of at least two-thirds of the several states have made applications on the same subject.

The project then set about a campaign to get petitions signed and recruit volunteers. As the organization of volunteers grows, more petitions get signed, and then volunteers become recruiters. The next step is for the volunteers to become lobbyists, advocating with their state legislators to sponsor a resolution.

Since the beginning of the Project in 2013, the number of supporters has grown dramatically, and numbers in the millions. Some supporters have done no more than sign the petition, about 5 million. Other supporters volunteer with a time commitment which varies dramatically, and makes them very hard to count. Some only show up at events once or twice a year, but talk to other people about the project in their every-day interactions. Others spend 15 or 20 minutes a few days a week making phone calls thanking people who have signed the petition. Still others set up booths at events of all kinds, gun shows, festivals, trade shows, political rallies, and conventions, anywhere people gather. Some spend untold hours in the halls of their state legislative offices building relationships with legislators and advocating for passage or continued support for existing resolutions. In all, they have become the largest grassroots organization in the nation. In October of 2022 they held a "gathering" in Orlando, Florida sponsored by the national organization. All travel and hotel expenses were borne by individual attendees, and the facilities were paid for with an attendance fee. There were over 600 people representing every state in the country.

In September of 2016, the national organization sponsored a "simulated convention" attended by state legislators from all over the country. The simulation adopted rules, formed committees, and proposed six amendments. This was certainly what Meckler called a "proof of concept", showing that the country could accomplish this bold objective.

In 2014, Georgia, Alaska, and Florida passed the resolution. Alabama joined with their resolution in 2015. Tennessee, Indiana, Oklahoma, and Louisiana passed resolutions in 2016. In 2017, Arizona, North Dakota, Texas, and Missouri passed resolutions. Arkansas, Utah, and Mississippi passed in 2019. In 2022, Wisconsin, Nebraska, West Virginia, and South Carolina passed resolutions. Although Oklahoma and Missouri both had automatic rescissions after five years, both replaced those applications with perpetual resolutions prior to the rescission.

In 2023, Kansas passed both chambers of the legislature with a wide majority vote, but there was a hitch. It seems that Kansas has a law requiring a two-thirds majority for this kind of resolution. That law is being challenged as unconstitutional both under the Kansas constitution and the U.S. Constitution.

The total number of states with the Convention of States Project application is now 19, or maybe 20 if we include Kansas. However, there is progress well beyond this. New Mexico, South Dakota, Iowa, Virginia, Wyoming, North Dakota, and New Hampshire have passed the resolution in one chamber, and the legislation is being actively pursued in following sessions. Connecticut, Michigan, and Pennsylvania have introduced legislation and passed a committee hearing. Colorado,

Hawaii, Illinois, Kentucky, Maine, Maryland, Massachusetts, Minnesota, Montana, New York, Rhode Island, Vermont, and Washington have all introduced legislation. So, beyond the 19 or 20 that have passed resolutions, there are another 23 or 24 with active legislation. This makes a total of 43 state legislatures debating the Convention of States Project resolution.

This resolution seeks to have a convention to propose amendments which limit the federal government in three key ways. First, to limit the power and jurisdiction, second to limit the fiscal resources, and third to limit the term in office. These areas of limitation would encompass many of the other resolutions we have reviewed such as repeal of the 16th amendment, the balanced budget amendment, apportionment or redistricting. There are some in the other groups that would also be covered here, such as the coercive use of funds, state control of education, review of supreme court decisions, debt limitation, and congressional term limits. Once again, the key is the popular self-governing, volunteer, activist role in this process. While the state legislators may be ambivalent, or even against the concept, they are being pressured by a growing number of their constituents who are becoming more and more insistent that they act. Very few politicians can withstand this pressure and expect to be reelected. With this grassroots army becoming more involved, the slow to act politician will surely face a popularly supported primary challenge as the number of active constituents grows.

Most recently, the Convention of States Foundation sponsored another "simulated" convention. This took place in Williamsburg, VA from August 2-4, 2023. There were over 100 people in attendance representing 49 states. Many of these simulated delegates are state representatives or senators. The result of this convention was six proposed amendments. In a real convention, these would require ratification of three-quarters, or 38, of the states. These six amendments were:

Proposal 1:

Section 1. No person shall be elected to serve in the House of Representatives more than nine full terms, nor elected or appointed to serve in the Senate more than three full terms. This article shall not disqualify any person from completing a term in the Congress to which that person was elected or appointed prior to ratification of this article.

Section 2. No person shall serve in the Congress for more than twenty-four years in total.

Proposal 2:

Section 1. The Supreme Court of the United States shall consist of nine judges, any six of whom shall constitute a quorum.

Section 2. Each of the several states shall have standing to bring an action challenging the constitutionality of any action of the Executive Branch or any enactment of Congress.

Proposal 3:

Section 1. Congress shall adopt a preliminary fiscal year budget no later than the first Monday in May for the following fiscal year and submit said budget to the President for consideration. Federal expenditures for each fiscal year shall not exceed average annual revenue collected in the prior three fiscal years. Total expenditures shall include all expenditures of the United States, including those for payment of interest on debt. Total revenue shall include all revenue of the United States except that derived from borrowing. Any surplus of revenue over expenditures in any fiscal year shall be applied to outstanding federal debt.

Section 2. Congress, whenever two thirds of both Houses of Congress by roll call vote deem it necessary, may exceed the spending limit in section one for one fiscal year by borrowing as provided for in the second clause of the eighth section of Article One of this Constitution.

Section 3. Taxes levied under the eighth section of Article One of this Constitution shall not be raised to increase the revenue of the United States unless two-thirds of both Houses of Congress by roll call vote concur.

Section 4. Nothing in this amendment shall be construed to allow for an increase in taxes without the express approval of Congress.

Section 5. This amendment will become effective three years after ratification.

Proposal 4:

Section 1. Commerce among the states shall mean buying, selling, or transportation of commercial goods and services across state lines.

Section 2. Congress shall not delegate any rule making function related to commerce among the states to any executive official or agency.

Section 3. Any federal law or regulation existing at the time of ratification of this amendment in conflict with this amendment shall become null and void two years after the date of ratification of this amendment.

Section 4. For purposes of this Constitution, Navigable Waters shall be limited to surface waters actively used for transport of goods in commerce among the states.

Proposal 5:

Section 1. The Legislatures of the States shall have authority to abrogate any action of Congress, President, or administrative agencies of the United States, whether in the form of a statute, decree, order, regulation, rule, opinion, decision, or other form. This provision shall not apply to presidential action taken pursuant to Article II, Section 2, Clause 1, and to presidential appointments.

Section 2. Such abrogation shall be effective when a simple majority of the Legislatures of the States declare the same provision or provisions of federal law to be abrogated. This abrogation authority may also be applied to provisions of federal law existing at the time this amendment is ratified. The state executive and judicial branches shall have no authority or involvement in this process.

Section 3. No government entity or official may take any action to enforce a provision of federal law after it is abrogated according to this Amendment. Any action to enforce a provision of abrogated federal law shall be enjoined by a federal or state court of general jurisdiction in the state where the enforcement action occurs, and costs and attorney fees of such injunction shall be awarded against the entity or official attempting to enforce the abrogated provision. Qualified and sovereign immunity shall not be available as a defense in such an action.

Section 4. No provision abrogated pursuant to this amendment may be reenacted or reissued in its original or substantially similar form for ten years from the date of the abrogation.

Proposal 6:

Section 1. Except with the permission of the Legislature of the State where the land is located, the national government shall not own, regulate, or control land or mineral rights, nor the proceeds from the sale of the same, except for the purposes expressly enumerated in Article I, Section 8, Clause 17.

Section 2. The national government shall not own, regulate, or control more than ten percent of the land and mineral rights in any given county or county equivalent, except with the express consent of the Legislature of the State in which the land is located, Article IV, Section 3, Clause 2 notwithstanding.

Section 3. Congress shall return or cede all remaining lands and mineral rights to the state in which it is located within ten years from the effective date hereof.

Section 4. For purposes of this Amendment, Control shall mean any combination of federal regulations, treaties, land use designations, and like measures which exert control over the land within a county and a State, which has the effect individually or in the aggregate of rendering all or any substantial portion of the land non-taxable, or renders the land unsusceptible to multiple use and sustained yield.

Section 5. This amendment shall not apply to lands or military installations with respect to which jurisdiction has been ceded to the United States by a State, lands belonging to an Indian or Indian tribe; or to lands that are designated as national parks, national monuments, or as congressionally designated wilderness as of January 1, 1976.

Section 6. For purposes of this Constitution, Navigable Waters shall be limited to surface waters actively used for transport of goods in interstate commerce.

Many of the attendees at this simulated convention were state legislators. Most of them have heard their constituents support this movement as activists in the largest grassroots army ever. Your opportunity to have an impact on the future of America may well be with this army. They are pressuring state legislatures in all fifty states to unleash the power of Article V.

The graph below shows the progress of the Convention of States Project:

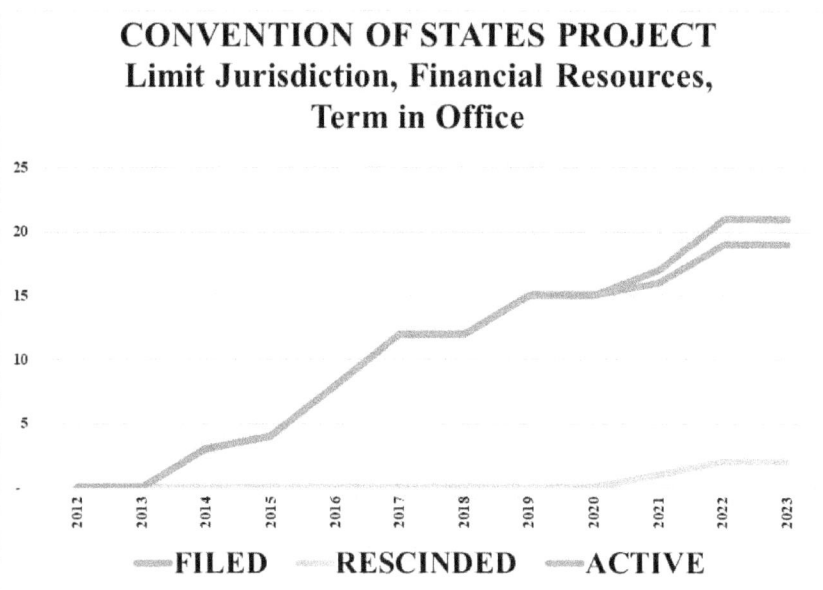

THE ALL-OTHER GROUP

So far, we have looked at those groups of applications containing the largest number of participating states having called for a convention on that subject matter since 1893. This incorporated 299 applications on 9 different subject matters, with 70 duplicates, 28 made moot by an amendment, 98 having been rescinded, leaving 103 active applications. We have not looked at the other 135 applications on 39 different subject matters, with 11 duplicates, 10 made moot by an amendment, 59 having been rescinded, leaving 55 active applications.

School Assignment –
During the school desegregation and bussing actions of the 1970s, 13 states made an application for a convention to limit the power of the federal government to assign kids to schools. These applications were filed between 1970 and 1978, and all but 4 have been rescinded.

Presidential Electors –
An anomaly of our Presidential election system, the electoral college allows for someone to be elected with a minority of the popular vote, so long as they garner a majority of the electoral vote. This has created controversy in several elections. Between 1957 and 1967 11 states filed applications for an amendment to revise the way electoral votes are allocated. Currently, most states have a winner take all allocation while a few allocate electoral votes based on the congressional district winners. All but six of these have been rescinded leaving five open.

Federal Taxing Power –
At the end of World War II, with federal spending and the national debt at an all time high, these applications sought to limit the taxing power of the federal government. These refer to both direct and indirect taxes. All 10 were submitted in 1944, and all but 4 have been rescinded.

Coercive Use of Federal Funds –
One way the federal government achieves its objectives outside its enumerated or even implied powers is to establish a "voluntary" program which state governments may participate in. The costs of such programs are paid for, sometimes overpaid for, with federal funds. The result is that state officials get to be the provider of a public benefit without the

stigma of having to raise taxes to pay for it. Soon, the program becomes a set of "golden handcuffs" on both the state officials and the people. Surprisingly, or maybe not, only eight of these were ever submitted, and sporadically between 1943 and 1994 and only 2 remain active.

Congressional Term Limits –
Term limiting Congress may feel like the most talked about subject in history. But yet, only 8 applications have been submitted between 1989 and 2023. In 1989 South Dakota filed an application for an Article V Convention for the purpose of a term limit amendment. Then in 1992 they joined 22 other states, who in the early 1990's had either passed laws or made state constitutional amendments which limited the terms of their congressional delegation. Many of these were the result of the state legislature lobbying efforts of the U.S. Term Limits organization. But in 1995, Arkansas politician Ray Thornton and others challenged the Arkansas law and took it all the way to the supreme court. In the 5-4 decision, the laws were found unconstitutional in U.S. Term Limits, Inc v. Thornton. U.S. Term Limits began working with state legislators to file more of these applications. Between 2016 and 2023 they have fostered the application through six state legislatures and have active legislation in seven other states.

World Federal Government –
These applications were looking for an amendment to allow negotiations with other nations in order to form a World Federal Government. If there is anything for opponents of the use of Article V to fear, this may well be it! These 7 applications, of which 3 are still open, were submitted between 1943 and 1949, and the United Nations may well be the result of the thought process which produced them, and that is bad enough. I can't imagine entering into a legitimate sharing of sovereignty with any other nation on earth. But for those who fear this result of an Article V Convention, let me say this. This would be a proposal only. It would require, like any other proposed amendment, be it from a convention or from congress, three-quarters of the states to ratify it. Remember the math of Justice Scalia? Only two percent of us can make any such proposed amendment fail! We should all be more concerned that this is happening extra-constitutionally in the bureaucracies in Washington one small step at a time as we argue!

State Control of Public Education –
As the debate raged over Brown v. Board of Education, these seven applications were submitted. More of us than ever agree that segregation laws are not good. However, we have witnessed how over the last 50 years with the Federal Department of Education established under President Carter and its growing influence on our local school systems, the degradation in the overall quality of education across the country. There is only one of these applications still open today.

Establish a Court of the Union –
These Five applications were all submitted in 1963. The Supreme Court decided many civil rights cases in this period, and many were controversial. Arkansas, Alabama, Florida, South Carolina, and Wyoming thought it would be a good idea to have a check on the Supreme Court. Their applications all spell out a proposed amendment where the highest justices of each state would form a "Court of the Union" and have the authority to review and overturn Supreme Court decisions. Three of these applications remain open today.

Selection and Tenure of Federal Judges –
Once again, dissatisfaction with the decisions of the Supreme Court had been a consistent state from the 1950s forward. These five applications were submitted between 1957 and 1981, all calling for a change in the way Supreme Court justices were selected, and seeking a limited term in office. Only one of these applications remains open.

Campaign Finance Reform –
After the decision on Citizens United was handed down, these five applications were submitted. They all called for some amendment to limit corporate money in political campaigns. These were championed by an organization known as Wolf – PAC. Four remain open today.

Unlimited –
There have been six applications between 1899 and 1929 submitted without any subject or reasoning indicated. These could be counted with any of the other applications or stand all by themselves. There are still four open today.

Limit Presidential Tenure –
These five applications were all submitted between 1943 and 1947, most likely in response to FDR's fourth term as President. They, of course, have been rendered moot by the ratification of the 22nd Amendment. All of them remain open today and if joined by 29 more could be used to change the presidential term limits again.

Repeal the 18th Amendment –
The American people just wanted a drink. Or, at least the legislators in five states did. These five applications remain open even though the 18th Amendment was repealed in 1933 by the 21st Amendment.

The remainder of the "All Other Group" have only had four or fewer applications ever submitted, and I will leave those in simple list form on the following page.

Subject Matter	Duplicate	Moot	Rescinded	Active	Total	Years
Antitrust	-	-	-	1	1	1911-1911
Constitutionality of state enactments	-	-	-	1	1	1913-1913
Taxation of bonds	-	-	2	1	3	1927-1970
Minimum Wage	-	-	-	1	1	1935-1935
Pensions for the elderly	-	-	-	2	2	1939-1964
World federal government	1	-	3	3	7	1943-1949
Coercive use of federal funds	-	-	6	2	8	1943-1994
Federal taxing power	-	-	8	2	10	1944-1994
Treaty making	-	-	2	1	3	1945-1957
Proceeds of federal taxes on fuel	-	-	-	1	1	1952-1952
State control of public education	2	-	4	1	7	1955-1965
Selection and tenure of federal judges	2	-	2	1	5	1957-1981
Supreme Court decisions	-	-	1	3	4	1957-2016
State taxing power over nonresidents	-	-	-	1	1	1958-1958
Federal preemption of state law	-	-	-	1	1	1959-1959
Validity 14th	-	-	-	1	1	1959-1959
Establish Court of the Union	-	-	2	3	5	1963-1963
Presidential electors	-	-	6	5	11	1963-1967
Federal/National debt limit	-	-	1	2	3	1963-2011
Control communism	-	-	-	1	1	1965-1965
School assignment	4	-	5	4	13	1970-1978
Funding private schools	2	-	-	2	4	1971-1974
VP Not Pres Senate	-	-	-	1	1	1972-1972
School prayer	-	-	3	1	4	1972-1973
Congressional term limits	-	-	2	6	8	1989-
Judicial authority	-	-	-	1	1	1993-1993
Posse Comitatus	-	-	-	1	1	2008-2008
Single Subject Matter	-	-	-	1	1	2014-2014
Campaign Finance Reform	-	-	1	4	5	2014-2016
Make All Federal Election Popular Vote	-	-	1	-	1	1901-1901
Repeal 18th	-	5	-	-	5	1925-1932
Limit presidential tenure	-	5	-	-	5	1943-1947
Oil and mineral rights	-	-	1	-	1	1957-1957
[unknown]	-	-	1	-	1	1960-1960
Sedition laws	-	-	1	-	1	1970-1970
Capital Punishment	-	-	1	-	1	1976-1976
Line-item veto	-	-	4	-	4	1977-1986
Federal regulations and rules	-	-	1	-	1	1979-1979
Flag desecration	-	-	1	-	1	1991-1991
Totals	11	10	59	55	135	

The next page shows all active applications by subject by state:

ACTIVE APPLICATIONS BY SUBJECT BY STATE

ACTIVE APPLICATIONS	ALL	FL	AL	MO	AR	IN	MS	IL	MI	NE	WI	CA	MA	PA	WY	IA	LA	ND	OH	AK	KY	NC	OR	RI	WA	AZ	CT	GA	KS	MN	NY	OK
Unlimited	4	X	X																													
Slavery	1	X																														
Clarify 10th	1		X																													
Balanced budget	26	X	X	X	X	X	X	X	X	X	X																						
COSPROJ	19	X	X	X	X	X	X	X																									
Apportionment	13	X	X	X		X		X	X	X				X	X	X		X															
Anti-polygamy	12	X	X	X	X	X	X	X		X			X																				
Right to life	10	X																															
Revenue sharing	9	X	X	X	X	X		X	X	X				X																			
Repeal 16th	8	X		X		X	X		X	X					X																		
Revision of Article V	6	X				X	X	X			X	X																					
Congressional term limits	6	X							X		X	X			X					X													
Presidential electors	5	X	X		X									X		X																	
School assignment	4								X	X																							
Campaign Finance Reform	4					X				X										X													X
World federal government	3												X	X																			
Supreme Court decisions	3		X	X														X															
Establish Court of the Union	3		X	X	X																												
Federal/National debt limit	2										X					X																	
Coercive use of federal funds	2			X											X																		
Federal taxing power	2									X									X														
Funding private schools	2																				X												
Pensions for the elderly	1							X																									
State control of public education	1									X													X										
Selection and tenure of federal judges	1		X											X																			
School prayer	1													X																			
Taxation of bonds	1						X						X																				
Treaty making	1			X					X																								
Antitrust	1																					X											
Control communism	1																											X					
Minimum Wage	1			X																													
Federal preemption of state law	1																											X					
State taxing power over nonresidents	1		X																														
VP Not President of Senate	1		X																														
Judicial authority	1			X																													
Single Subject Matter	1		X																														
Validity 14th	1																																
Constitutionality of state enactments	1					X							X																				
Posse Comitatus	1																															X	
Proceeds of federal taxes on fuel	1			X																						X							X
TOTAL	164	11	10	10	9	9	9	7	6	6	6	5	5	5	5	4	4	4	4	3	3	3	3	3	3	2	2	2	2	2	2	2

FIRST 105 YEARS
BOOK CHAPTERS
ALL OTHERS

THE LIBERTY AMENDMENT

These applications have been included in the "Repeal the 16th Amendment" section and count. Their story, however, is of particular importance to the subject following this discussion.

Willis Emerson Stone was born on July 20, 1899. He was a descendant of Ralph Waldo Emerson and of a signer of the Declaration of Independence, Thomas Stone. He was mostly an industrial engineer but had been a realtor, advertising executive, and newspaper reporter for portions of his life. He retired in 1958 to dedicate his life to achieving an amendment to the U.S. Constitution.

In his newspaper column on June 2, 1944, Mr. Stone recommended an amendment to the Constitution to restrain federal powers. The amendment he recommended was similar to Section 1 of what is now the Liberty Amendment. The most current version, as presented to the consideration of congress in 2011, and identical to the five state applications for an article V convention, reads as follows (*106 Cong. Rec. 14,401, 1960, 106 Cong. Rec. 10,749, 1960, 125 Cong. Rec. 12,287, 1979, 108 Cong. Rec. 5051, 1962, 105 Cong. Rec. 3085-86, 1959*):

Section 1. The Government of the United States shall not engage in any business, professional, commercial, financial, or industrial enterprise except as specified in the Constitution.

Section 2. The constitution or laws of any State, or the laws of the United States, shall not be subject to the terms of any foreign or domestic agreement which would abrogate this amendment.

Section 3. The activities of the United States Government which violate the intent and purposes of this amendment shall, within a period of three years from the date of the ratification of this amendment, be liquidated and the properties and facilities affected shall be sold.

Section 4. Three years after the ratification of this amendment the sixteenth article of amendments to the Constitution of the United States shall stand repealed and thereafter Congress shall not levy taxes on personal incomes, estates, and gifts.

The amendment was introduced initially as a single section which incorporated sections 1 – 3 above in 1952 by Representative Ralph W. Gwinn (R – NY).

June 28, 1952 Congressional Record – House, (98 Cong. Rec. 8542, 1952):

By Mr. GWINN: H. J. Res. 491. Joint resolution proposing an amendment to the Constitution of the United States relative to calling of a convention to consider an amendment to the Constitution to prohibit the United States Government from engaging in business in competition with its citizens; to the Committee on the Judiciary.

It was reintroduced in congress in 1953, 1955, and in 1957. In 1957 a separate resolution was introduced to repeal the 16th amendment. On June 10, 1957, Representative Elmer J. Hoffman (R – IL) added the repeal of the 16th amendment as section 4 to the Liberty Amendment and introduced it as a single amendment.

As noted above, Willis Stone had retired in 1958 to promote the Liberty Amendment. He founded the National Committee for Economic Freedom in 1959 with the sole purpose of promoting his amendment. He established affiliated committees in each state and was the chairman.

Also in 1959, Wyoming became the first state to submit an application for the Liberty Amendment (which I counted as a duplicate to their 1939 application for repeal of the 16th amendment). In that application, they do three things. First, they endorse the Liberty amendment which Representative James Utt (R – CA) had introduced in congress. Second, they asked congress to submit that amendment to the states for ratification. Third, they made a formal application for an article V convention to propose the amendment. Louisiana and Nevada submitted identical applications (also counted in the repeal of the 16th amendment section) in 1960. Texas passed a resolution endorsing the Liberty Amendment in 1960, but made no application for a convention. Georgia did the same in 1962. South Carolina submitted an identical application in 1962. In 1963 an article V resolution in Alabama for the application had passed the House and was pending in the Senate, but the session ended and the resolution died.

During this time, the Virginia Commission on Constitutional Government began working to publish an anthology of historic documents and commentaries on the constitution. In 1963 they published their work in a document entitled "We the States" (Library of Congress Catalog No 64-23522). The conclusions of their work resulted in their complete and full support of the Liberty Amendment. Perhaps the most telling phrase in their document was "even to the most casual eye, the house of our fathers has fallen into decay. The great beams that gave it strength – the separation of powers within the central government, the division of responsibility between the States and the Federal authority – are tending to crumble under subtle and insidious attack". Today, under the blatant attacks, an archeologist would be hard pressed to find real evidence that those strong beams ever existed at all.

Mr. Stone changed the name of his organization in 1963 to "The Liberty Amendment of the USA" to better identify the sole purpose. By that time there were active State Committees in 47 states. Their work to promote the amendment, both in congress and in state legislatures continued with little results for the next ten years.

In 1973, Representative John Rarick (D – LA), also an Advisory Board member to the Committee, introduced the amendment in congress. In 1975, Representative John Rousselot (R – CA) introduced the amendment. One of its most fervent supporters was Larry McDonald (D – GA), and also a member of the John Birch society since the mid 60's, gave a 30-minute testimony on the floor of the house on October 9, 1975. He started by explaining how many questions he had been asked about the Liberty Amendment and formatted his testimony in the form of answers to more than 70 questions. He included an excellent explanation of how article V provided for amendments to be proposed by both the congress and the states, and that in the end, the states held the key to ratification but needed to be included from the beginning.

The proposed amendment was introduced in congress in 1977 by John Rousselot (R – CA), in 1978 by James Collins (R – TX) in 1978, Rousselot and Collins in 1979, Rousselot in 1981, Ron Paul (R – TX) in 1983, 1998, 1999, 2001, 2004, 2005, 2009, and in 2011. In 1983, Larry McDonald co-sponsored the resolution, and also became Chairman of the John Birch Society. In September of 1983, McDonald was aboard KAL Flight 007 when it was shot down by a Russian MIG. Willis Emerson Stone died in 1989.

In 1979, Arizona submitted their application for the Liberty Amendment. In 1982 Indiana and Mississippi passed resolutions endorsing the amendment. So, while the Liberty Amendment went on being ignored every time it was introduced in the halls of congress, the states quit thinking about it after 1979. The high point of this concept was either five States submitting applications for an article V convention or the testimony of Larry McDonald in 1975.

OBJECTION TO USE OF ARTICLE V CONVENTION

As with anything dealing with legislation, government or politics, there will be objections. Most of the time these objections deal with being on one side or the other of an issue under debate. Our constitution sets up the control mechanisms for these debates to be carried out in as orderly and respectful manner as possible. This is done through the separation of powers and the checks and balances employed.

For example, we may argue vehemently that the President should not have vetoed our favored bill, but we rarely argue that he should never use his veto. We may truly dislike the fact that the Senate failed to confirm a particular Supreme Court appointee, but almost never that they should not avail themselves of that power. We almost always have heated debates on a 5 to 4 Supreme Court decision, or whether they had jurisdiction to hear that particular case but rarely about their appropriate use of the powers granted in article III.

We even have debates about whether any branch or any level of government should have the power it is exercising, or for that matter that it should have powers not yet granted to it. We argue ad nauseam about whether a particular clause in the constitution grants this or that power. We rarely make an argument that a clear power identified in the constitution should simply be ignored and never utilized. Our constitution grants and limits all of the powers of the federal government. We have clearly seen in the prior chapters that the federal government exceeds those powers on a regular basis. We argue that limits are being ignored and that someone should do something about it.

That, in fact, is the precise reason for the existence of Article V in our constitution. It is there to grant more powers, or to impose more limits, or clarify the precise meaning of the powers already granted the federal government. Yet there exists a few who argue that this power should never be used. Remember, this is not an argument on how and when it may or may not be appropriate to use. It's not an objection to a particular solution that may be proposed through the exercise of the amendment power. It is an argument that the amendment power should never be used, or at least that the Article V convention option should never be employed.

There are two main conservative organizations which are dedicated to the prevention of an article V convention being held no matter what. These are the John Birch Society (JBS), and the Eagle Forum. The liberal left has opponents to proposing amendments which reduce federal power, but in fact have some organizations who are pushing for a convention to propose left leaning amendments, but haven't really seen success in the measure of applications submitted. This is how it's supposed to work; we all compete for consensus, and sometimes we win, and sometimes we lose.

Nearest I have been able to determine, is that the common denominator for JBS and Eagle Forum, both in a single person and overall timing is a woman named Phyllis Schlafly. She was a force to be reckoned with when it came to conservative causes. She ran for congress in 1952 but lost. In 1957 she and her husband wrote the "American Bar Association's Report on Communist Tactics, Strategy, and Objectives". Over the course of the 60's and 70's she appeared everywhere but mostly in the fight against the Equal Rights Amendment. She was a member of the John Birch Society and in 1972 founded the Eagle Forum. She has a very long and distinguished resume, and I encourage you to read more about her.

Sometime in 1988, she inquired of Chief Justice Warren Burger as to his thoughts on an Article V convention. He responded with this letter:

June 22, 1988

Dear Phyllis:

I am glad to respond to your inquiry about a proposed Article V Constitutional Convention. I have been asked questions about this topic many times during my news conferences and at college meetings since I became Chairman of the Commission on the Bicentennial of the U.S. Constitution, and I have repeatedly replied that such a convention would be a grand waste of time.

I have also repeatedly given my opinion that there is no effective way to limit or muzzle the actions of a Constitutional Convention. The Convention could make its own rules and set its own agenda. Congress might try to limit the Convention to one amendment or to one issue, but there is no way to assure that the Convention would obey. After a Convention is convened, it will be too late to stop the Convention if we don't like its agenda. The meeting in 1787 ignored the limit placed by the Confederation Congress "for the sole and express purpose."

With George Washington as chairman, they were able to deliberate in total secrecy, with no press coverage and no leaks. A Constitutional Convention today would be a free-for-all for special interest groups, television coverage, and press speculation.

Our 1787 Constitution was referred to by several of its authors as a "miracle." Whatever gain might be hoped for from a new Constitutional Convention could not be worth the risks involved. A new Convention could plunge our Nation into constitutional confusion and confrontation at every turn, with no assurance that focus would be on the subjects needing attention. I have discouraged the idea of a Constitutional Convention, and I am glad to see states rescinding their previous resolutions requesting a Convention. In these Bicentennial years, we should be celebrating its long life, not challenging its very existence. Whatever may need repair on our Constitution can be dealt with by specific amendments.

You may find this letter at:
https://www.phyllisschlafly.com/wp-content/uploads/2020/02/Con-Con-Article-V-Warren-Burger-letter.pdf

It is clear that Chief Justice Burger was not a fan of the convention method to propose amendments.

I believe that it is this letter which sent both the John Birch Society and the Eagle Forum into full combat mode on avoidance of an Article V Convention.

The John Birch Society was founded by Robert Welch in 1958 with its main objective being to combat communism. Larry McDonald was his successor at the helm of JBS in 1983. As reviewed in the Liberty

Amendment section, both worked diligently to work the amendment through both congress and state legislatures calling for an Article V convention. It is my belief that this mission took a 180 degree turn under pressure from Phyllis Schlafly after her receipt of Justice Berger's reply above. She took the Justices words as gospel and indelibly imprinted them on both JBS and Eagle Forum. Over the last 35 years these organizations have been working diligently to get states to rescind their calls for a convention. They have amassed an impressive array of experts who agree with the convention disaster projection.

I want to take the Burger concerns one at a time:
- The Convention could make its own rules and set its own agenda.
- Congress might try to limit the Convention to one amendment or to one issue, but there is no way to assure that the Convention would obey.
- After a Convention is convened, it will be too late to stop the Convention if we don't like its agenda.
- The meeting in 1787 ignored the limit placed by the Confederation Congress "for the sole and express purpose."
- A Constitutional Convention today would be a free-for-all for special interest groups, television coverage, and press speculation.
- A new Convention could plunge our Nation into constitutional confusion and confrontation at every turn, with no assurance that focus would be on the subjects needing attention.

Point 1. The Convention Will Make Its Own Rules and Set Its Own Agenda.

Yes, the convention delegates will do what all conventions do. They will make rules, determine officers and committees and a few other administrative tasks. They will look to see if there are ready made rules to work from, just like all of the previous Conventions of States including the Constitutional Convention (rules in the appendix), the Convention of States Project simulation in Virginia, (rules in the appendix), and the BBA Task Force convention in Arizona (rules in the appendix). The agenda will be set by the charge the delegates are given by their state legislatures. At least 11 states have laws governing how that will happen. No part of Article V, or the rest of the Constitution is there granted a rule making authority. Perhaps Chief Justice Burger was most concerned that he did not get to write the rules or set the agenda?

Point 2. Congress might try to limit the Convention to one amendment or to one issue, but there is no way to assure that the Convention would obey.

We have seen in the review of applications submitted by the states that they will try to limit the subjects addressed by the convention through the wording of their applications. What we have yet to see is how Congress will word its call with respect to the wording of states applications. We have not seen that yet because Congress may be in dereliction of their duty.

Professor Michael Paulsen has perhaps looked hardest into the subject of limiting the scope of an Article V Convention should it be called. In his paper from 1993 "A General Theory of Article V: The Constitutional Lessons of the Twenty-seventh Amendment" contains an insightful review of the applications as of that date (see link below).
https://openyls.law.yale.edu/bitstream/handle/
20.500.13051/8800/32_103YaleLJ677_December1993_.pdf?
sequence=2&isAllowed=y.

I believe I understand him to say that states may, in an application for an article V convention, suggest a topic for attention, but if they use the "sole or exclusive" language that it invalidates the application. He bases this assertion on the fact that Article V does not specify the ability of the states to limit the convention. I would assert that neither does Article V prohibit the states from doing so. He also argues that the Congress may not limit the scope in their call because Article V doesn't say they can. I once again would argue that neither does it say they can't. There is no doubt that the convention delegates may limit the subjects they debate; after all, they will make the rules by which they operate.

Perhaps the best response is the last paragraph and last sentence of the Paulsen article:

The fears sometimes expressed about giving Article V its natural reading are fears that, despite Article V's very difficult gauntlet of formal hurdles and abundance of procedural checks, the amendment process will be too easy and too much out of the hands of Congress or the courts - that is, too much in the hands of the People themselves. This is especially true of the specter of a second constitutional convention. But that is exactly why the Constitution does not place the amendment process exclusively under the control of politicians and judges. The People are the ultimate source of all legitimate government power and can be trusted with the mechanisms they have been bequeathed for altering or abolishing their form of government, with or without the consent of those who presently govern them. Certainly, the People can be entrusted with the management of the amendment process as written by the Framers, and not be forced to accept some revision written for the benefit of their overlords.

https://openyls.law.yale.edu/bitstream/handle/
20.500.13051/8800/32_103YaleLJ677_December1993_.pdf?
sequence=2&isAllowed=y

Would the President, Congress and Supreme Court, and its Chief Justice qualify as overlords? Do we run in fear from the promise of Article V because our overlords say we should?

Beyond the question of whether Congress may not limit the subjects addressed in convention, the states most certainly will. Some may argue that once the convention is underway, neither the states nor Congress may control the proceedings. This ignores the efforts many states have made in preparation for this eventuality. At least eleven states, Arkansas, Florida, Georgia, Indiana, Louisiana, South Dakota, Tennessee, Texas, Utah, Wisconsin, and Wyoming have state laws controlling how delegates will be selected and what authority they will be given. Most have in place an unfaithful delegate law and many attach a felony crime as well. With delegates so managed, it is hard to imagine a run away from whatever the states may choose to call the purpose of the convention, never mind what Congress may or may not have indicated in their call, if they ever make one.

Point 3. After a Convention is convened, it will be too late to stop the Convention if we don't like its agenda.

Who is "we" that might like to stop the Convention because "we" don't like the agenda? It seems to me that Berger is pointing out that the federal government, that is the court, or Berger, can't control the Convention. Absolutely not!! This convention is under the auspices of state legislatures through their duly assigned and charged delegates. However much Berger would like to control it, that is not his job, and he should not have the power to do anything but watch. That goes for any part of the federal government.

Point 4. The meeting in 1787 ignored the limit placed by the Confederation Congress "for the sole and express purpose."

The 1787 convention did ignore the Confederation Congress "for the sole and express purpose" instructions in the call. First, the Confederation Congress did not have any authority in the Articles of Confederation to call a convention or limit a convention if it was called by a particular state, which is what actually happened. After the failed Annapolis convention of 1786, the Commissioners sent a letter to 13 states and the Congress, calling for the Philadelphia convention without the words "sole and express purpose".

The commissioners from the Annapolis convention, which only five states attended, sent a full report to all 13 states and the Continental Congress dated September 14, 1786. In that report, they made this invitation (Kaminski, J.P. et al., 2009):

..... in the appointment of Commissioners, to meet at Philadelphia on the second Monday in May next, to take into consideration the situation of the United States, to devise such further provisions as shall appear to them necessary to render the constitution of the Foederal Government adequate to the exigencies of the Union.

On November 23rd, 1786, Virginia appointed seven Commissioners with instructions to meet in Philadelphia in (Kaminiski, J. P. et al., 2009):
devising and discussing all such alterations and further provisions, as may be necessary to render the Federal Constitution adequate to the exigencies of the Union;

On November 24th, 1786 New Jersey empowered delegates to meet in Philadelphia for the purpose of (Kaminiski, J. P. et al., 2009):
taking into consideration the state of the Union as to trade and other important objects, and of devising such further provisions as shall

appear necessary to render the Constitution of the federal government adequate to the exigencies thereof

On December 30th, 1786, Pennsylvania's General Assembly appointed deputies to meet with those authorized from other states in (Kaminiski, J. P. et al., 2009):
devising, deliberating on, and discussing all such alterations and further provisions as may be necessary to render the foederal constitution fully adequate to the exigencies of the Union;

On January 6th, 1787, North Carolina authorized delegates to meet with delegates of other states to (Kaminiski, J. P. et al., 2009):
discuss and decide upon the most effectual means to remove the defects of our foederal union

On February 3rd, 1787, Delaware appointed deputies instructed to meet with those appointed by other states in (Kaminiski, J. P. et al., 2009):
devising, deliberating on, and discussing, such Alterations and further Provisions, as may be necessary to render the Foederal Constitution adequate to the Exigencies of the Union

On February 10th, 1787, Georgia appointed deputies to meet delegates authorized by other states in (Kaminiski, J. P. et al., 2009):
devising and discussing all such alterations and farther provisions, as may be necessary to render the federal constitution adequate to the exigencies of the union
Before Congress did anything on the subject, Virginia had made the invitation, and five states had already responded to Virginia's invitation and reasons to meet in Philadelphia. Virginia had no sole and express language in its invitation, nor did the five states who had already identified and charged delegates with authority.

On February 21st, 1787, the Confederation Congress proposed an invitation which failed to carry and then approved a second proposed invitation which read (Jensen, M. et al., eds., 1976, 185–88):
"Resolved that in the opinion of Congress it is expedient that on the second Monday in May next a convention of delegates who shall have been appointed by the several states be held at Philadelphia for the sole and express purpose of revising the Articles of Confederation and reporting to Congress and the several legislatures such alterations and

provisions therein as shall when agreed to in Congress and confirmed
by the states render the federal constitution adequate to the exigencies
of government and the preservation of the Union."

Congress had no authority in the Articles of Confederation to make an independent call of a convention, nor to limit in any way the actions of such a convention. Congress' call to meet in Philadelphia is then a courtesy based upon the report of the commissioners from the Annapolis convention and no more. The addition of the "sole and express purpose of revising the Articles of Confederation" has no authority. Moreover, since none of the six states had included the phrase in the charge to their delegates, nor did the invitation from the Annapolis commissioners, it carries no weight. Madison's notes of the same day indicate that the change was made by delegates from New York and Massachusetts who were unfriendly to the concept of a convention, and many considered the resolution a deadly blow to the existing confederation.

On February 26th through 28th, the New York Assembly and Senate debated the sending of delegates to the proposed convention. The Assembly, on the 26th, approved a resolution with the language "for the sole and express purpose of revising the Articles of Confederation". The next day, the Senate resolved that they did not concur with the Assembly, and made alteration to the number and mode of election of delegates but kept the language of sole and express purpose. On the 28th, the Assembly concurred and the final language directed delegates to meet (Kaminiski, J. P. et al., 2009):

for the sole and express purpose of revising the Articles of
Confederation, and reporting to Congress and to the several legislatures
such alterations and provisions therein as shall when agreed to in
Congress and confirmed by the several states, render the federal
constitution adequate to the exigencies of government and the
preservation of the Union.

On March 7th through the 9th, Massachusetts debated their sending delegates and ended up with near identical language as New York (Kaminiski, J. P. et al., 2009):

for the sole & express purpose of revising the articles of Confederation,
and reporting to Congress & the several Legislatures, such alterations &
provisions therein, as shall when agreed to in Congress, and confirmed
by the States, render the federal Constitution adequate to the exigences

of Government & the preservation of the Union.

But then the Senate added more limitations, instructing delegates that they were (Kaminiski, J. P. et al., 2009):
not to accede to any alterations or additions that may be proposed to be made in the present Articles of Confederation, which may appear to them, not to consist with the true republican Spirit and Genius of the Said Confederation: and particularly that they by no means interfere with the fifth of the Said Articles which provides, "for the annual election of Delegates in Congress, with a power reserved to each State to recall its Delegates, or any of them within the Year & to send others in their stead for the remainder of the year— And which also provides, that no person shall be capable of being a Delegate for more than three years in any term of six years, or being a Delegate shall be capable of holding any Office under the United States for which he or any other for his benefit, receives any salary, fees, or emolument of any kind".

On March 8th, 1787, South Carolina instructed its selected delegates to meet in Philadelphia, and that they were (Kaminiski, J. P. et al., 2009):
duly authorized and impowered in devising and discussing all such alterations, clauses, articles and provisions as may be thought necessary to render the foederal constitution entirely adequate to the actual situation and future good government of the confederated states.

May 14th, 1787, was the second Monday in May next referred to in the Annapolis Commissioners invitation. Some state delegations had arrived, but seven would be required to make a quorum.

On May 17th, 1787, Connecticut appointed its delegates and empowered them to (Kaminiski, J. P. et al., 2009):
discuss upon such Alterations and Provisions, agreeable to the general Principles of Republican Government, as they shall think proper, to render the foederal Constitution adequate to the Exigencies of Government, and the Preservation of the Union

On May 25th, a quorum of states was present, and the convention was called to order.

On May 26th, 1787, Maryland appointed their deputies to meet in Philadelphia (Kaminiski, J. P. et al., 2009):
for the purpose of revising the federal system, and to join with them in considering such alterations, and further provisions, as may be necessary to render the federal constitution adequate to the exigencies of the union.

On June 27th, 1787, New Hampshire became the 12th and last state to appoint delegates to (Kaminiski, J. P. et al., 2009):
discuss and decide upon the most effectual means to remedy the defects of our federal union.

So it was that only two states and Congress, with no power to do so, called for the limitation of "sole and express purpose" of amending the Articles. All of the other states empowered delegates to recommend what seemed to them to be the best solution to the issues at hand. The outcome was a recommended new Constitution, along with a specific mode of ratification. No state was obliged to do anything with this recommendation. The Articles of Confederation were still intact and in full force, and still not working to mediate tensions between the several states. The delegates to the convention all comported themselves completely in keeping with the authority granted them by their respective states. New York and Massachusetts delegates did not officially participate by vote in any of the proceedings once their mandates were exceeded. James Madison argues this very point in Federalist Number 40.

Chief Justice Berger's assertion that the delegates ignored the limit placed on the convention is correct, but the premise that the Confederation Congress had the authority to limit the convention is wrong. The state legislatures were the ones which controlled the proceedings through the authority given to their appointed delegates. Authority which may have differed slightly from state to state, but was consistent enough to allow the convention to reach its legitimate conclusion. If Berger argues that the convention's actions were illegitimate, then the conclusion, our constitution, is also illegitimate and has no power.

Point 5. A Constitutional Convention today would be a free-for-all for special interest groups, television coverage, and press speculation.

Yes, special interest groups always prevail. Right now, they are prevailing on the floor of congress, in the oval office, in every bureaucratic agency of the federal government and most state governments. Special interest groups prevail with the election of every President and his appointments to the Supreme Court and therefore to the rulings they ultimately hand down. None of the officials involved, elected, appointed or hired, are under any state law as the delegates will be at convention.

I would go further, and argue that special interest groups prevailed in Philadelphia in the summer of 1787 as well. There were the slaveholding planters of the Carolinas, Georgia and Virginia. There were the merchants of Philadelphia, New York and Boston. There were the shipping magnates with large international trading interests. There were the delegates from the most populous states and the smaller states, with aspirations of great power and fear of being trod upon respectively. Those special interest groups prevailed in creating a form of government workable for people who don't like each other. That, in fact, is the "miracle" Chief Justice Burger is pointing to, not the control of Congress, the President or the Court. Is he truly arguing that we are to fear the power of the people?

This special interest group fear is a fear based on their influence to use a proposed amendment to expand federal power in their favor. Of the 315 applications reviewed in the 10 subjects of most note, 8 of the subjects encompassing 234 applications seek to place limits on federal power. The Direct election of Senators did not expand federal power, nor did it protect state power with its 60 applications. I'll argue that the Anti-Polygamy subject would have expanded federal power in that it is limiting individual rights. The vast majority of the subjects in The All-Other Group also seek to limit federal power. So, to fear an expansion of federal power from a group of delegates under significant control of state legislatures seeking to limit that power is an unfounded fear.

Point 6. A new Convention could plunge our Nation into constitutional confusion and confrontation at every turn, with no assurance that focus would be on the subjects needing attention.

Isn't the nation in a continuous state of constitutional confusion as it is? The federal government has grown to such ungainly proportions with so many different rule-making (law) bodies that each of us is likely guilty of at least one felony per day. So many people today have no clue how our government is supposed to work. Very few understand the appropriate relationship between themselves and the federal vs. the state governments, let alone the appropriate relationship between the federal and state governments. I am convinced that we will be no more constitutionally confused after an Article V convention, and have a high likelihood of being less so if it works as anticipated by the founders and the current proponents.

So, in conclusion to the objections to an Article V Convention made by Chief Justice Berger and expanded out of all proportion by Mrs. Schlafly, the JBS and the Eagle Forum we see only fear---understandable fear, but fear none the less. Perhaps I am more afraid of what will happen if we don't use every option to put the federal government back in check, than I am of any particular option going wrong.

More importantly, are "we the people" supposed to sit idly and let our government become despotic? Our role in self-governance is clear. This letter and the support of the John Birch Society and the Eagle Forum are calculated to make you fear the specter of state legislatures assigning delegates to use a constitutional method of removing federal powers. Our government should be more afraid of us than we are of it. Berger was clearly afraid of the people, hence his vehement assertion that he would be unable to control them. That is exactly what we want him to be afraid of!

To my friends in the JBS and Eagle Forum organizations, I ask you to put away your fear and add your voice to the growing number of voices who want to put the states and the people back in control of the federal government.

MICHAEL PAULSEN CRITERIA

After the surprise ratification of the 27th amendment in 1992, constitutional scholar Michael Paulsen set out to count Article V applications. After all, if a 202-year-old proposed amendment can suddenly be ratified, is an Article V Convention less plausible? Article V requires that two-thirds of the states make an application to congress for a convention. His inquiry was to see how many states had applied, and not rescinded in order to reach the threshold.

You may read his resulting article here:
https://openyls.law.yale.edu/bitstream/handle/
20.500.13051/8800/32_103YaleLJ677_December1993_.pdf?
sequence=2&isAllowed=y

It must have been an arduous search for and review of state resolutions, both applications for an article V convention, and rescissions of previous applications. I have benefited from all of these being available at: http://articlevlibrary.com/applications.htm which was not available to him. After this search, review and application of his deep constitutional scholarship, he presents a few key rules on how to count applications.

He cites Professors Charles Black and Walter Dellinger as contending that a convention may not be limited by a specific proposal or subject matter, or for that matter limited at all. They contend that any application suggesting subject limitations is invalid.

He then cites Professor William Van Alstyne and others contending that the convention may be limited. In March of 1979, Professor Van Alstyne, in fact, responded with a letter to Professor Bruce Ackerman with respect to the position of Professor Black. His assertion is that the contemplation of Article V was that a particular issue would, in fact, be the cause for states to submit applications for a convention. In his letter he says (Van Alstyne, W. W., 1978, Faculty Publications Paper 803):

"To put the matter simply, a generous construction of what suffices to present a valid application by a state, for consideration of a particular subject or of a particular amendment in convention, is far more responsive to the anticipated uses of article V than a demanding

construction that all but eliminates its use in response to specific, limited state dissatisfactions."

He also makes the very valid point that (Van Alstyne, W. W., 1978, Faculty Publications Paper 803):

"certain kinds of amendments state legislatures might wish to have considered by a convention would be precisely the kinds least likely to be forthcoming from Congress - indeed, the very kinds to which Congress could be expected to be hostile."

The entire letter is well worth the read and may be downloaded here: https://papers.ssrn.com/sol3/papers.cfm?abstract_id=1983224

Professor Paulsen contends that there are two questions, 1) can the convention be limited, and 2) is an application with a subject matter valid? His answer to the first is that a convention, once convened, is a free agency and may propose whatever it likes, and further that Congress is bound to submit what it proposes to the states for ratification, and therefore, a convention may NOT be limited. His answer to the second question is that applications with subject limitations need to be looked at in two parts. First, absent language specifically making the application contingent on the limiting of the convention, the subject is just a suggestion, and the application is valid. Second, an application with language which makes it contingent on the convention being limited is invalid. These words would be "sole and exclusive" or "limited to". He bases his invalidation argument on the contention that the state's application may not limit Congress' actions.

While Professor Paulsen is a constitutional scholar and I'm just an old, fat, bald accountant, I respectfully disagree, and am in complete agreement with Professor Van Alstyne. I base my disagreement on the fact that Article V does not specifically require or prohibit a limit being set by either the states or Congress. Since the state is not limited in how it words an application, and if it has words that express a desire for Congress to call a convention under Article V, then it is an application. Since Congress is not limited by anything except the requirement to call a convention upon two-thirds of the states making an application, and every application counts, then that is what Congress must do. Further, Congress may word its call however it sees fit, no limit, or a specifically worded amendment. But the convention is a free agency once convened and will do as it pleases. I believe that what it will be pleased to do is to follow the laws of the states which sent them to the convention, at least eleven of which are very specific as to the selection, instructions, recall of delegates, and the punishment for unfaithful delegates. But in particular, what of the case where there are thirty-four substantially the same applications with specific limiting language? Congress, the states, and the delegates would have very little to stand on in claiming plenary powers.

Paulsen's next rule is that based on the number and timing of a state's applications and rescissions, the state's light is either "on" for an Article V Convention, or, it is "off", having no active applications. So, a state with one or several un-rescinded applications light remains "on" and countable to reach the magical two-thirds.

The last rule is that based on any point in time, if the number of states with their lights "on" with any number of applications without the dreaded "sole and exclusive", or "limited to", language is 34 or greater, then Congress is under an obligation to call a convention. Of course, my rule pays no attention to the limiting language.

Paulsen determined that Congress had been, for a long period of time, under an obligation to call a convention by the mandate in Article V. In 1993 there were just under 400 applications on file with some having been rescinded, and others expressing the dreaded "sole and exclusive" language. The 50 plus applications created since his analysis all contain limiting language.

Here are the statistics. Of the 450 applications in existence, 272 are not limited, it's hard to be sure on 12, and 168 contain limiting language. Of the 272 not limited, 148 have not yet been rescinded. The 148 valid and in force applications belong to 30 states. So today, 30 states have their lights on under the Paulsen criteria. Compare this to the 40 states with their lights on when you count those which include limits.

The following page contains a graph showing how many states each year had their lights "on", based on the Paulsen criteria as compared to the threshold number of states to trigger the call for a convention. Keep in mind that the Paulsen criteria rules out any application with the words "sole and exclusive". If we include those un-rescinded applications, we get a very different view of Congress' obligation to call an Article V Convention.

The orange line on the graphs represents two-thirds of the states as the number of states grew from 13 to 50, and the two-thirds level grew from 9 to 34. The blue line on the graphs represents the number of states with their lights "on" in each year.

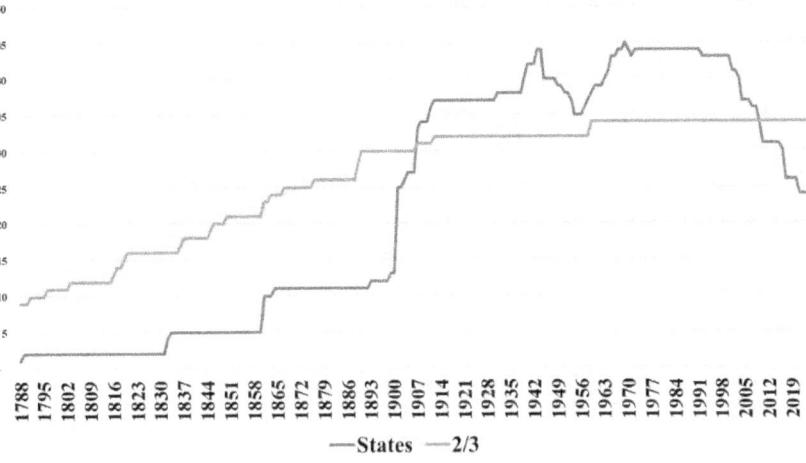

Paulsen Criteria States With Lights "ON"

Based on the Paulsen criteria, Congress was under an obligation to call an Article V Convention from 1907 through 2008. If we allow for limited applications to count as a "light is on" status for a state, the graph below indicates that Congress remains under an obligation to call an Article V Convention today.

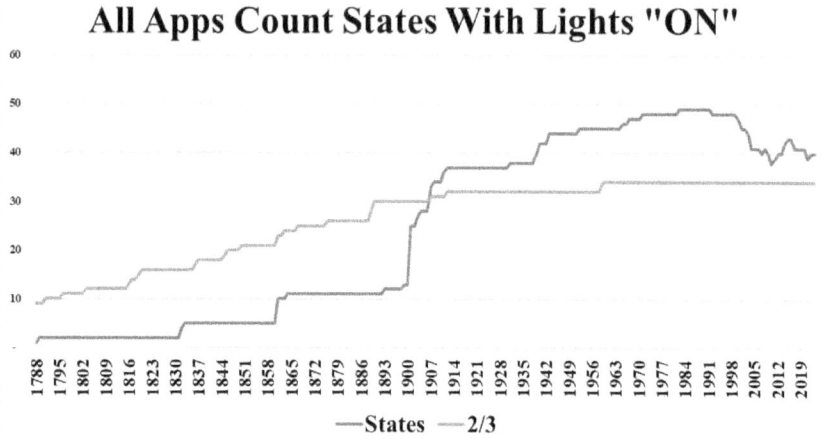

All Apps Count States With Lights "ON"

—States —2/3

WHEN WILL CONGRESS ACT?

We now arrive at the real questions which desperately need answers. But first let's review the relevant part of Article V:
"..or on the application of two-thirds of the several states, [Congress] shall call a convention for proposing amendments...."

What counts as an application under Article V?

The language makes no condition on what constitutes an application, or, for that matter, what invalidates it from being an application. Therefore, any resolution submitted to Congress containing the words which in plain english say it's an application under Article V for a convention to propose amendments, it must qualify. Period. Any other words in the resolution may be a signal that a subject, or specific amendment language, is all that a state's delegate may participate in, or vote on, but it does not limit the document from being an application. Congress has 450 of these in its possession from 49 states.

Paulsen makes a foolproof argument that a legislature may make a resolution, and then later rescind that resolution, after which it is like the original resolution never existed. He also argues that if a resolution is part of a group that reaches a predetermined threshold, it cannot be rescinded after that threshold has been reached. Under this logic, an application may be rescinded prior to there being 34 states with unrescinded applications, the threshold, but not after. That threshold was reached in 1907. Further, if all unrescinded applications count, Congress is still under that obligation today. Under the Paulsen criteria of disqualified applications, Congress was relieved of that duty in 2009 with rescissions of applications.

To the opponents of the Article V Convention effort who fear that Congress will take over at the first opportunity, why have they not done so for 116 years? If Congress shirks its duty and does not call a convention what happens? The real answer is, nothing. If Congress has neglected an opportunity to take over a convention, then the fears of the opponents are unfounded. If, as Paulsen insists, applications can not be limited, then Congress has been shirking its duty since 1907, so, nothing, is in fact the answer.

Surely, Congress would not intentionally shirk their Constitutionally Mandatory Duty. Would they?

That answer is a resounding YES!! As it turns out, John James Blaine (1875 – 1934) was the U.S. Senator from Wisconsin from 1927 to 1934. On two separate occasions, September 4th and September 23rd, 1929, he laid before the Senate two different resolutions from the Wisconsin Legislature calling on Congress to do its Constitutionally Mandated Duty, since 35 states had applied for an Article V Convention, and the two-thirds threshold at the time was 32 states. By my count, 1929 had 37 states with open applications, and I have determined that the Wisconsin Legislature missed applications from South Carolina and West Virginia. Both of Blaine's resolutions were referred to the Judiciary Committee where they died. The resolutions are identical, but they were both submitted and read into the record separately:

September 4, 1929 Cong. Rec. Vol 71, p. 3369 ("Senate Joint Resolution 65")

September 23, 1929 Cong. Rec. Vol 71, p. 3856 ("Senate Joint Resolution 83")

The VICE PRESIDENT also laid before the Senate the following joint resolutions of the Legislature of the State of Wisconsin, which were referred to the Committee on the Judiciary:
STATE OF WISCONSIN.

Senate Joint Resolution 65.

Joint resolution memorializing the Congress of the United States to discharge the mandatory duties imposed upon it by Article V of the Constitution of the United States to call a convention to propose amendments to the Constitution

Whereas the legislatures of the following 35 States have filed a formal application with Congress to call a convention for the purpose of proposing amendments to the Constitution of the United States: Alabama, Arkansas, California, Colorado, Delaware, Georgia, Idaho, Illinois, Indiana, Iowa, Kansas, Kentucky, Louisiana, Maine, Michigan, Minnesota, Missouri, Montana, Nebraska, Nevada, New Jersey, New

York, North Carolina, Ohio, Oklahoma, Oregon, Pennsylvania, South Dakota, Tennessee, Texas, Utah, Vermont, Virginia, Washington, and Wisconsin ; and

Whereas Article V of the Constitution of the United States reads as follows : " The Congress, whenever two-thirds of both Houses -shall deem it necessary, shall propose amendments to this Constitution, or, on the application of the legislatures of two-thirds of the several States, shall call a convention for proposing amendments, which, in either case, shall be valid to all intents and purposes, as part of this Constitution, when ratified by the legislatures of three-fourths of the several States, or by conventions in three-fourths thereof, as the one or the other mode of ratification may be proposed by the Congress: Provided, That no amendment which may be made prior to the year 1808 shall in any manner affect the first and fourth clauses in the ninth section of the first article; and that no State, without its consent, shall be deprived of its equal suffrage in the Senate " ; and

Whereas this article makes it mandatory upon the Congress of the United States to call a convention for the purpose of proposing amendments to the Constitution whenever two-thirds of the States shall have made application therefor: Now, therefore, be it

Resolved by the senate (the assembly concurring), That the Legislature of the State of Wisconsin respectfully requests that the Congress of the United States perform the mandatory duty imposed upon it by, the above-quoted Article V and forthwith call a convention to propose amendments to the Constitution of the United States; be it further

Resolved, that properly attested copies of this resolution be transmitted to the presiding officers of both Houses of the Congress of the United States and to each Wisconsin Member thereof.

HENRY A. HUBER, President of the Senate.
O.G. MUNSON, Chief Clerk of the Senate
Chas. B. Ferry, Speaker of the Assembly
C.E. Shaffer, Chief Clerk of the Assembly

Perhaps a better question than, "what is an application?", would be, "who decides when the two-thirds threshold is met?". Since meeting the threshold puts the ball in Congress' court, then Congress must act. Deciding not to act, or ignoring the controlling fact that they must act, does not imply that Congress has the final say. I would assert that when the threshold is met is a provable fact, the convening of a Convention is required, independent of Congress' dereliction of their duty to act.

Perhaps Congress insists that if an application contains a stated purpose, then it only counts with other applications containing substantially the same stated purpose. That must be the case since Congress would surely deny that they have shirked their Constitutionally mandated duty. So, Congress is waiting patiently for an application with substantially the same subject as 33 others before they act.

Further, if Congress insists that the applications contain substantially the same stated purpose, then a limit to that stated purpose should have no effect on the validity of that application. Applications with "sole and exclusive" or, "sole purpose" or, "limited to" are actually fulfilling what Congress must see as the requirement, not an invalidation of the application.

The conclusion here is that Congress believes that States may limit the convention to particular subjects is a limit on the Constitutional requirement that they must call a convention. If that is the case, then what would the resolution calling the convention look like? In keeping with the apparent belief that the States may limit the convention, then their resolution should also limit the convention to that same subject as the 34 State resolutions.

What is Congress doing in this area? Well, most recently Senator Mike Braun (R-IN) and Representative Jodey Arrington (R-TX) have filed some interesting bills.

Jodey Arrington led the way in July of 2022 when he filed two bills. He filed HCR 101 which called for congress to call an Article V Convention, and HR 8419 which called for the National Archives administrator to count and publish all Article V Applications. Both of these went to the Judiciary Committee to die and be buried along with those of Senator Blaine from 1929. He resurrected HCR 101 and filed in 2023 as HCR 24 and it appears to be on life support in the Judiciary Committee as well.

Senator Mike Braun picked up Arrington's HR 8419 from the grave and filed it anew as S.810. This fresh bill calls for the Senate and the House of Representatives to (1) make Article V Application submissions available online in a searchable format that is organized by state of origin and year of submission; and (2) provide certain information about each submission, including whether the submission proposes a new amendment or rescinds a prior proposal and the citation for the submission in the Congressional Record. That sounds a whole lot like www.articlevlibrary.com. This looks to be headed to the Congressional morgue as well.

It seems that Congressman Arrington does not believe the states may limit the convention, and that the two-thirds threshold has been met.

Senator Braun seems to want a documented list which can be reviewed by everyone. It may be presumed that from this review a debate and a consensus may be formed as to both the question of subject matter aggregation, and the two-thirds threshold.

However, in each case, Congress as a whole seems to be ignoring the Article V question entirely. Perhaps they are shirking their constitutional duty after all.

When the ball is in Congress' court, and they refuse to pick it up, what then? Let's look at Madison's words in Federalist 85:

The intrinsic difficulty of governing thirteen States at any rate, independent of calculations upon an ordinary degree of public spirit and integrity, will, in my opinion, constantly impose on the national rulers the necessity of a spirit of accommodation to the reasonable expectations of their constituents. But there is yet a further consideration, which proves beyond the possibility of a doubt, that the observation is futile. It is this that the national rulers, whenever nine States concur, will have no option upon the subject. By the fifth article of the plan, the Congress will be obliged "on the application of the legislatures of two thirds of the States (which at present amount to nine), to call a convention for proposing amendments, which shall be valid, to all intents and purposes, as part of the Constitution, when ratified by the legislatures of three fourths of the

States, or by conventions in three fourths thereof." The words of this article are peremptory. The Congress "shall call a convention." Nothing in this particular is left to the discretion of that body. And of consequence, all the declamation about the disinclination to a change vanishes in air. Nor however difficult it may be supposed to unite two thirds or three fourths of the State legislatures, in amendments which may affect local interests, can there be any room to apprehend any such difficulty in a union on points which are merely relative to the general liberty or security of the people. We may safely rely on the disposition of the State legislatures to erect barriers against the encroachments of the national authority.

Nothing in this particular is left to the discretion of that body.

We may safely rely on the disposition of the State legislatures to erect barriers against the encroachments of the national authority.

The federal government which has authority to do 30 or so jobs has over 400 federal agencies doing so much more. Of the 30 jobs delegated to them, they are failing miserably to perform. Federal agencies run rough-shod over the administration. Congress seems incapable of any actions except spending money and incurring more and more debt. The judiciary is a tangled mess of political activism.

Article V was put into the Constitution for a time such as this. We are born and raised in a country which espouses the right to self-governance. The states have great power in Article V. The people have the ability to influence their state legislatures much more than they have so far. The greater the numbers of people pressuring state legislators, the greater their political will to use the power of Article V.

The unleashing of that great power is the only route to restore power usurped by the federal government back to the states and the people.

I assert that Article V is a power valve which allows Congress to ask for more power, and the states to suggest reducing that power. The states may reduce the federal power by proposing and ratifying amendments which clarify the meaning of the words in the Constitution. The subject matter contained within the applications indicate the ways in which the states would like to alter the power of the federal government.

The subjects and potential amendments in those applications matter. Congress may not be obligated to give any credit to suggested limits on the convention. But when or if Congress calls a convention with or without limits, the States may or may not be obligated to empower their delegates with those same limits. Whatever charge the States give their delegates will be the most control that may be exerted on the convention processes and outcomes. The outcomes of the convention will be proposed amendments. Nothing about the Constitution changes because of a proposed amendment either from Congress or an Article V Convention. In the end, States have the final say in the ratification process.

I believe wholeheartedly that some proposed amendments which limit federal power are desperately needed. Let's look at the 450 applications submitted by the states from the point of view of limiting federal power. Some seek to Limit, some seek to Expand, and some are unclear as to their effect. I have assigned one of these criteria to each of the 450 applications, and to each of the 52 subjects, and the 42 active subjects and the results are:

Effect	apps	active apps	subj	active subj
limiting	299	115	31	26
expanding	70	38	14	11
unclear	81	11	7	5
total	450	164	52	42

I will also note that I have included as expanding federal power the applications for the subjects of Anti-Polygamy, Right to Life, and Slavery. I see the first two as necessary goals for a family-oriented society to achieve. Outlawing slavery is obvious and certainly key in protecting liberty. But allocating these items to the federal government control expands that federal power. Each of them can be accomplished by the state government without any federal oversight. The intent of our original Constitution was to grant the federal power to accomplish things that no state could do adequately on its own.

It is clear that the vast majority of the applications and subjects have the state legislatures wanting to limit some aspect of the federal power. This may well be the disincentive for Congress to perform its Constitutionally Mandated Duty and call an Article V convention. This would be true in the event that Congress believes that subject does not matter in determining the two-thirds threshold, or that subjects suggested by States must be aggregated in determining the threshold. Congress will not propose an amendment limiting its power, nor will they call a convention curtailing the subject matter it contemplates to those limiting Congressional power.

If Congress will not perform a task which is not left to its discretion, and we are left to rely on the disposition of state legislatures to erect barriers against these encroachments, what barrier is it? The Constitutional barrier must be built with Article V. It is the only tool likely to be effective in overcoming the federal encroachments of the last 130 years.

CONCLUSION

If you are a State Legislator, I thank you for reading this far. I also ask you to take the next step and join with your colleagues in calling for an Article V resolution which will ultimately pass any measure of the two-thirds threshold. Join in the Balanced Budget Amendment applications, or the Term Limit applications, or the Convention of States applications which are certainly being discussed in your legislature. If your state already has applications on file, reach out to State Legislators in other states. You could form a coalition of legislators across state lines working together to erect that barrier our country so desperately needs. I wrote this book in the belief that when fully armed with historical information, an urgent appeal from your constituents and finding like minded fellow legislators you would be more committed and more effective.

If you are a concerned citizen of one of these United States, or already already an activist for limited government, then this book is also for you. I have met many who want to be active in shaping the future of local, state, and federal governments. Not very many are as effective as they could be. Many activists are single cause focused. Many understand the particular legislation they would like to promote at a high level, but get caught up in one liners and platitudes which seem to support their cause and then fall apart when challenged.

In writing this book, I have arrived at a new understanding of the breadth and depth of this subject, and even a greater understanding of how much I still have to learn. Most of all, I have learned that those focused on state and local government reforms and legislation would find their jobs much easier without the existence of some federal legislation, funding, regulations or guidelines. The purpose of state proposed Article V amendments is to eliminate those very obstacles to your success.

I challenge you to look for the type of amendment which would remove those federal regulations in your way to achieving your state or local goals. Then join the many Article V supporters across the country to apply pressure on your state legislator to support that kind of Article V resolution.

We the people, each of us as a citizen of one of the United States of America, have an awesome power to combine our efforts and make our voices heard and our desires felt. We have an obligation to retain the gift of liberty and to guarantee that it is passed to our posterity. I implore you to get involved. You owe it, like I do, to ourselves, our children, our grand-children, and our great-grand-children.

Use this knowledge, the history of constitutional change. Let it be empowering to you to help shape the future of America. Be a part of unleashing Article V.

Offer
Author is available for speaking engagements.

Let's Connect

LinkedIn

Facebook QR

APPENDICES

The following pages are appendices referred to in the foregoing text

Appendix 1 - Full Text of the U.S. Constitution and 27 Amendments - https://constitutioncenter.org/the-constitution/full-text

Appendix 2 - Full Text of the Articles of Confederation https://www.archives.gov/milestone-documents/articles-of-confederation

Appendix 3 - Balanced Budget Amendment Task Force Rules Package https://www.azleg.gov/alispdfs/BBAPC/ Convention_Resolution_1_Engrossed.pdf

Appendix 4 - 1787 Constitutional Convention Rules https://teachingamericanhistory.org/document/the-rules-of-the-convention/

Appendix 5 - Convention of States Simulated Convention Rules https://d3n8a8pro7vhmx.cloudfront.net/conventionofstates/pages/6429/ attachments/original/1474237364/simulation_rules_final3.pdf? 1474237364

APPENDIX 1 - U.S. CONSTITUTION

We the People of the United States, in Order to form a more perfect Union, establish Justice, insure domestic Tranquility, provide for the common defence, promote the general Welfare, and secure the Blessings of Liberty to ourselves and our Posterity, do ordain and establish this Constitution for the United States of America.

Article I

Section 1: The Congress

All legislative Powers herein granted shall be vested in a Congress of the United States, which shall consist of a Senate and House of Representatives.

Section 2: The House of Representatives

The House of Representatives shall be composed of Members chosen every second Year by the People of the several States, and the Electors in each State shall have the Qualifications requisite for Electors of the most numerous Branch of the State Legislature.

No Person shall be a Representative who shall not have attained to the Age of twenty-five Years, and been seven Years a Citizen of the United States, and who shall not, when elected, be an Inhabitant of that State in which he shall be chosen.

Representatives and direct Taxes shall be apportioned among the several States which may be included within this Union, according to their respective Numbers, which shall be determined by adding to the whole Number of free Persons, including those bound to Service for a Term of Years, and excluding Indians not taxed, three fifths of all other Persons. The actual Enumeration shall be made within three Years after the first Meeting of the Congress of the United States, and within every subsequent Term of ten Years, in such Manner as they shall by Law direct. The number of Representatives shall not exceed one for every thirty Thousand, but each State shall have at Least one Representative; and until such enumeration shall be made, the State of

New Hampshire shall be entitled to chuse three, Massachusetts eight, Rhode-Island and Providence Plantations one, Connecticut five, New-York six, New Jersey four, Pennsylvania eight, Delaware one, Maryland six, Virginia ten, North Carolina five, South Carolina five, and Georgia three.

When vacancies happen in the Representation from any State, the Executive Authority thereof shall issue Writs of Election to fill such Vacancies.

The House of Representatives shall chuse their Speaker and other Officers and shall have the sole Power of Impeachment.

Section 3: The Senate

The Senate of the United States shall be composed of two Senators from each State, chosen by the Legislature thereof, for six Years; and each Senator shall have one Vote.

Immediately after they shall be assembled in Consequence of the first Election, they shall be divided as equally as may be into three Classes. The Seats of the Senators of the first Class shall be vacated at the Expiration of the second Year, of the second Class at the Expiration of the fourth Year, and of the third Class at the Expiration of the sixth Year, so that one third may be chosen every second Year; and if Vacancies happen by Resignation, or otherwise, during the Recess of the Legislature of any State, the Executive thereof may make temporary Appointments until the next Meeting of the Legislature, which shall then fill such Vacancies.

No Person shall be a Senator who shall not have attained to the Age of thirty Years, and been nine Years a Citizen of the United States, and who shall not, when elected, be an Inhabitant of that State for which he shall be chosen.

The Vice President of the United States shall be President of the Senate, but shall have no Vote, unless they be equally divided.

The Senate shall chuse their other Officers, and also a President pro tempore, in the Absence of the Vice President, or when he shall exercise the Office of President of the United States.

The Senate shall have the sole Power to try all Impeachments. When sitting for that Purpose, they shall be on Oath or Affirmation. When the President of the United States is tried, the Chief Justice shall preside: And no Person shall be convicted without the Concurrence of two thirds of the Members present.

Judgment in Cases of Impeachment shall not extend further than to removal from Office, and disqualification to hold and enjoy any Office of honor, Trust or Profit under the United States: but the Party convicted shall nevertheless be liable and subject to Indictment, Trial, Judgment and Punishment, according to Law.

Section 4: Elections

The Times, Places and Manner of holding Elections for Senators and Representatives, shall be prescribed in each State by the Legislature thereof; but the Congress may at any time by Law make or alter such Regulations, except as to the Places of chusing Senators.

The Congress shall assemble at least once in every Year, and such Meeting shall be on the first Monday in December, unless they shall by Law appoint a different Day.

Section 5: Powers and Duties of Congress

Each House shall be the Judge of the Elections, Returns and Qualifications of its own Members, and a Majority of each shall constitute a Quorum to do Business; but a smaller Number may adjourn from day to day, and may be authorized to compel the Attendance of absent Members, in such Manner, and under such Penalties as each House may provide.

Each House may determine the Rules of its Proceedings, punish its Members for disorderly Behaviour, and, with the Concurrence of two thirds, expel a Member.

Each House shall keep a Journal of its Proceedings, and from time to time publish the same, excepting such Parts as may in their Judgment require Secrecy; and the Yeas and Nays of the Members of either House on any question shall, at the Desire of one fifth of those Present, be entered on the Journal.

Neither House, during the Session of Congress, shall, without the Consent of the other, adjourn for more than three days, nor to any other Place than that in which the two Houses shall be sitting.

Section 6: Rights and Disabilities of Members

The Senators and Representatives shall receive a Compensation for their Services, to be ascertained by Law, and paid out of the Treasury of the United States. They shall in all Cases, except Treason, Felony and Breach of the Peace, be privileged from Arrest during their Attendance at the Session of their respective Houses, and in going to and returning from the same; and for any Speech or Debate in either House, they shall not be questioned in any other Place.

No Senator or Representative shall, during the Time for which he was elected, be appointed to any civil Office under the Authority of the United States, which shall have been created, or the Emoluments whereof shall have been increased during such time; and no Person holding any Office under the United States, shall be a Member of either House during his Continuance in Office.

Section 7: Legislative Process

All Bills for raising Revenue shall originate in the House of Representatives; but the Senate may propose or concur with Amendments as on other Bills.

Every Bill which shall have passed the House of Representatives and the Senate, shall, before it become a Law, be presented to the President of the United States; If he approve he shall sign it, but if not he shall return it, with his Objections to that House in which it shall have originated, who shall enter the Objections at large on their Journal, and proceed to reconsider it. If after such Reconsideration two thirds of that House shall agree to pass the Bill, it shall be sent, together with the

Objections, to the other House, by which it shall likewise be reconsidered, and if approved by two thirds of that House, it shall become a Law. But in all such Cases the Votes of both Houses shall be determined by Yeas and Nays, and the Names of the Persons voting for and against the Bill shall be entered on the Journal of each House respectively. If any Bill shall not be returned by the President within ten Days (Sundays excepted) after it shall have been presented to him, the Same shall be a Law, in like Manner as if he had signed it, unless the Congress by their Adjournment prevent its Return, in which Case it shall not be a Law.

Every Order, Resolution, or Vote to which the Concurrence of the Senate and House of Representatives may be necessary (except on a question of Adjournment) shall be presented to the President of the United States; and before the Same shall take Effect, shall be approved by him, or being disapproved by him, shall be repassed by two thirds of the Senate and House of Representatives, according to the Rules and Limitations prescribed in the Case of a Bill.

Section 8: Powers of Congress

The Congress shall have Power To lay and collect Taxes, Duties, Imposts and Excises, to pay the Debts and provide for the common Defence and general Welfare of the United States; but all Duties, Imposts and Excises shall be uniform throughout the United States;

To borrow Money on the credit of the United States;

To regulate Commerce with foreign Nations, and among the several States, and with the Indian Tribes;

To establish a uniform Rule of Naturalization, and uniform Laws on the subject of Bankruptcies throughout the United States;

To coin Money, regulate the Value thereof, and of foreign Coin, and fix the Standard of Weights and Measures;

To provide for the Punishment of counterfeiting the Securities and current Coin of the United States;

To establish Post Offices and post Roads;

To promote the Progress of Science and useful Arts, by securing for limited Times to Authors and Inventors the exclusive Right to their respective Writings and Discoveries;

To constitute Tribunals inferior to the supreme Court;

To define and punish Piracies and Felonies committed on the high Seas, and Offenses against the Law of Nations;

To declare War, grant Letters of Marque and Reprisal, and make Rules concerning Captures on Land and Water;

To raise and support Armies, but no Appropriation of Money to that Use shall be for a longer Term than two Years;

To provide and maintain a Navy;

To make Rules for the Government and Regulation of the land and naval Forces;

To provide for calling forth the Militia to execute the Laws of the Union, suppress Insurrections and repel Invasions;

To provide for organizing, arming, and disciplining, the Militia, and for governing such Part of them as may be employed in the Service of the United States, reserving to the States respectively, the Appointment of the Officers, and the Authority of training the Militia according to the discipline prescribed by Congress;

To exercise exclusive Legislation in all Cases whatsoever, over such District (not exceeding ten Miles square) as may, by Cession of particular States, and the Acceptance of Congress, become the Seat of the Government of the United States, and to exercise like Authority over all Places purchased by the Consent of the Legislature of the State in which the Same shall be, for the Erection of Forts, Magazines, Arsenals, dock-Yards and other needful Buildings; -And

To make all Laws which shall be necessary and proper for carrying into Execution the foregoing Powers, and all other Powers vested by this Constitution in the Government of the United States, or in any Department or Officer thereof.

Section 9: Powers Denied Congress

The Migration or Importation of such Persons as any of the States now existing shall think proper to admit, shall not be prohibited by the Congress prior to the Year one thousand eight hundred and eight, but a Tax or duty may be imposed on such Importation, not exceeding ten dollars for each Person.

The Privilege of the Writ of Habeas Corpus shall not be suspended, unless when in Cases of Rebellion or Invasion the public Safety may require it.

No Bill of Attainder or ex post facto Law shall be passed.

No Capitation, or other direct, Tax shall be laid, unless in Proportion to the Census or Enumeration herein before directed to be taken.

No Tax or Duty shall be laid on Articles exported from any State.

No Preference shall be given by any Regulation of Commerce or Revenue to the Ports of one State over those of another: nor shall Vessels bound to, or from, one State, be obliged to enter, clear, or pay Duties in another.

No Money shall be drawn from the Treasury, but in Consequence of Appropriations made by Law; and a regular Statement and Account of the Receipts and Expenditures of all public Money shall be published from time to time.

No Title of Nobility shall be granted by the United States: And no Person holding any Office of Profit or Trust under them, shall, without the Consent of the Congress, accept of any present, Emolument, Office, or Title, of any kind whatever, from any King, Prince, or foreign State.

Section 10: Powers Denied to the States

No State shall enter into any Treaty, Alliance, or Confederation; grant Letters of Marque and Reprisal; coin Money; emit Bills of Credit; make any Thing but gold and silver Coin a Tender in Payment of Debts; pass any Bill of Attainder, ex post facto Law, or Law impairing the Obligation of Contracts, or grant any Title of Nobility.

No State shall, without the Consent of the Congress, lay any Imposts or Duties on Imports or Exports, except what may be absolutely necessary for executing it's inspection Laws: and the net Produce of all Duties and Imposts, laid by any State on Imports or Exports, shall be for the Use of the Treasury of the United States; and all such Laws shall be subject to the Revision and Controul of the Congress.

No State shall, without the Consent of Congress, lay any Duty of Tonnage, keep Troops, or Ships of War in time of Peace, enter into any Agreement or Compact with another State, or with a foreign Power, or engage in War, unless actually invaded, or in such imminent Danger as will not admit of delay.

Article II

Section 1

The executive Power shall be vested in a President of the United States of America.

He shall hold his Office during the Term of four Years, and, together with the Vice President, chosen for the same Term, be elected, as follows:

Each State shall appoint, in such Manner as the Legislature thereof may direct, a Number of Electors, equal to the whole Number of Senators and Representatives to which the State may be entitled in the Congress: but no Senator or Representative, or Person holding an Office of Trust or Profit under the United States, shall be appointed an Elector.

The Electors shall meet in their respective States, and vote by Ballot for two Persons, of whom one at least shall not be an Inhabitant of the same State with themselves. And they shall make a List of all the Persons voted for, and of the Number of Votes for each; which List they shall sign and certify, and transmit sealed to the Seat of the Government of the United States, directed to the President of the Senate. The President of the Senate shall, in the Presence of the Senate and House of Representatives, open all the Certificates, and the Votes shall then be counted. The Person having the greatest Number of Votes shall be the President, if such Number be a Majority of the whole Number of Electors appointed; and if there be more than one who have such Majority, and have an equal Number of Votes, then the House of Representatives shall immediately chuse by Ballot one of them for President; and if no Person have a Majority, then from the five highest on the List the said House shall in like Manner chuse the President. But in chusing the President, the Votes shall be taken by States, the Representation from each State having one Vote; A quorum for this Purpose shall consist of a Member or Members from two thirds of the States, and a Majority of all the States shall be necessary to a Choice. In every Case, after the Choice of the President, the Person having the greatest Number of Votes of the Electors shall be the Vice President. But if there should remain two or more who have equal Votes, the Senate shall chuse from them by Ballot the Vice President.

The Congress may determine the Time of chusing the Electors, and the Day on which they shall give their Votes; which Day shall be the same throughout the United States.

No Person except a natural born Citizen, or a Citizen of the United States, at the time of the Adoption of this Constitution, shall be eligible to the Office of President; neither shall any person be eligible to that Office who shall not have attained to the Age of thirty five Years, and been fourteen Years a Resident within the United States.

In Case of the Removal of the President from Office, or of his Death, Resignation, or Inability to discharge the Powers and Duties of the said Office, the Same shall devolve on the Vice President, and the Congress may by Law provide for the Case of Removal, Death, Resignation or Inability, both of the President and Vice President, declaring what Officer shall then act as President, and such Officer shall act accordingly, until the Disability be removed, or a President shall be elected.

The President shall, at stated Times, receive for his Services, a Compensation, which shall neither be increased nor diminished during the Period for which he shall have been elected, and he shall not receive within that Period any other Emolument from the United States, or any of them.

Before he enter on the Execution of his Office, he shall take the following Oath or Affirmation:--"I do solemnly swear (or affirm) that I will faithfully execute the Office of President of the United States, and will to the best of my Ability, preserve, protect and defend the Constitution of the United States."

Section 2

The President shall be Commander in Chief of the Army and Navy of the United States, and of the Militia of the several States, when called into the actual Service of the United States; he may require the Opinion, in writing, of the principal Officer in each of the executive Departments, upon any Subject relating to the Duties of their respective Offices, and he shall have Power to grant Reprieves and Pardons for Offenses against the United States, except in Cases of Impeachment.

He shall have Power, by and with the Advice and Consent of the Senate, to make Treaties, provided two thirds of the Senators present concur; and he shall nominate, and by and with the Advice and Consent of the Senate, shall appoint Ambassadors, other public Ministers and Consuls, Judges of the supreme Court, and all other Officers of the United States, whose Appointments are not herein otherwise provided for, and which shall be established by Law: but the Congress may by Law vest the Appointment of such inferior Officers, as they think proper, in the President alone, in the Courts of Law, or in the Heads of Departments.

The President shall have Power to fill up all Vacancies that may happen during the Recess of the Senate, by granting Commissions which shall expire at the End of their next Session.

Section 3

He shall from time to time give to the Congress Information of the State of the Union, and recommend to their Consideration such Measures as he shall judge necessary and expedient; he may, on extraordinary Occasions, convene both Houses, or either of them, and in Case of Disagreement between them, with Respect to the Time of Adjournment, he may adjourn them to such Time as he shall think proper; he shall receive Ambassadors and other public Ministers; he shall take Care that the Laws be faithfully executed, and shall Commission all the Officers of the United States.

Section 4

The President, Vice President and all civil Officers of the United States, shall be removed from Office on Impeachment for, and Conviction of, Treason, Bribery, or other high Crimes and Misdemeanors.

Article III

Section 1

The judicial Power of the United States, shall be vested in one supreme Court, and in such inferior Courts as the Congress may from time to time ordain and establish. The Judges, both of the supreme and inferior Courts, shall hold their Offices during good Behaviour, and shall, at stated Times, receive for their Services, a Compensation, which shall not be diminished during their Continuance in Office.

Section 2

The judicial Power shall extend to all Cases, in Law and Equity, arising under this Constitution, the Laws of the United States, and Treaties made, or which shall be made, under their Authority;--to all Cases affecting Ambassadors, other public Ministers and Consuls;--to all Cases of admiralty and maritime Jurisdiction;--to Controversies to which the United States shall be a Party;--to Controversies between two or more States;--between a State and Citizens of another State;--between

Citizens of different States;--between Citizens of the same State claiming Lands under Grants of different States, and between a State, or the Citizens thereof, and foreign States, Citizens or Subjects.

In all Cases affecting Ambassadors, other public Ministers and Consuls, and those in which a State shall be Party, the supreme Court shall have original Jurisdiction. In all the other Cases before mentioned, the supreme Court shall have appellate Jurisdiction, both as to Law and Fact, with such Exceptions, and under such Regulations as the Congress shall make.

The Trial of all Crimes, except in Cases of Impeachment; shall be by Jury; and such Trial shall be held in the State where the said Crimes shall have been committed; but when not committed within any State, the Trial shall be at such Place or Places as the Congress may by Law have directed.

Section 3

Treason against the United States, shall consist only in levying War against them, or in adhering to their Enemies, giving them Aid and Comfort. No Person shall be convicted of Treason unless on the Testimony of two Witnesses to the same overt Act, or on Confession in open Court.

The Congress shall have Power to declare the Punishment of Treason, but no Attainder of Treason shall work Corruption of Blood, or Forfeiture except during the Life of the Person attainted.

Article IV

Section 1

Full Faith and Credit shall be given in each State to the public Acts, Records, and judicial Proceedings of every other State. And the Congress may by general Laws prescribe the Manner in which such Acts, Records and Proceedings shall be proved, and the Effect thereof.

Section 2

The Citizens of each State shall be entitled to all Privileges and Immunities of Citizens in the several States.

A Person charged in any State with Treason, Felony, or other Crime, who shall flee from Justice, and be found in another State, shall on Demand of the executive Authority of the State from which he fled, be delivered up, to be removed to the State having Jurisdiction of the Crime.

No Person held to Service or Labour in one State, under the Laws thereof, escaping into another, shall, in Consequence of any Law or Regulation therein, be discharged from such Service or Labour, but shall be delivered up on Claim of the Party to whom such Service or Labour may be due.

Section 3

New States may be admitted by the Congress into this Union; but no new State shall be formed or erected within the Jurisdiction of any other State; nor any State be formed by the Junction of two or more States, or Parts of States, without the Consent of the Legislatures of the States concerned as well as of the Congress.

The Congress shall have Power to dispose of and make all needful Rules and Regulations respecting the Territory or other Property belonging to the United States; and nothing in this Constitution shall be so construed as to Prejudice any Claims of the United States, or of any particular State.

Section 4

The United States shall guarantee to every State in this Union a Republican Form of Government, and shall protect each of them against Invasion; and on Application of the Legislature, or of the Executive (when the Legislature cannot be convened) against domestic Violence.

Article V

The Congress, whenever two thirds of both Houses shall deem it necessary, shall propose Amendments to this Constitution, or, on the Application of the Legislatures of two thirds of the several States, shall call a Convention for proposing Amendments, which, in either Case, shall be valid to all Intents and Purposes, as Part of this Constitution, when ratified by the Legislatures of three fourths of the several States, or by Conventions in three fourths thereof, as the one or the other Mode of Ratification may be proposed by the Congress; Provided that no Amendment which may be made prior to the Year One thousand eight hundred and eight shall in any Manner affect the first and fourth Clauses in the Ninth Section of the first Article; and that no State, without its Consent, shall be deprived of its equal Suffrage in the Senate.

Article VI

All Debts contracted and Engagements entered into, before the Adoption of this Constitution, shall be as valid against the United States under this Constitution, as under the Confederation.

This Constitution, and the Laws of the United States which shall be made in Pursuance thereof; and all Treaties made, or which shall be made, under the Authority of the United States, shall be the supreme Law of the Land; and the Judges in every State shall be bound thereby, any Thing in the Constitution or Laws of any State to the Contrary notwithstanding.

The Senators and Representatives before mentioned, and the Members of the several State Legislatures, and all executive and judicial Officers, both of the United States and of the several States, shall be bound by Oath or Affirmation, to support this Constitution; but no religious Test shall ever be required as a Qualification to any Office or public Trust under the United States.

Article VII

The Ratification of the Conventions of nine States, shall be sufficient for the Establishment of this Constitution between the States so ratifying the Same.

First Amendment

Congress shall make no law respecting an establishment of religion, or prohibiting the free exercise thereof; or abridging the freedom of speech, or of the press; or the right of the people peaceably to assemble, and to petition the Government for a redress of grievances.

Second Amendment

A well regulated Militia, being necessary to the security of a free State, the right of the people to keep and bear Arms, shall not be infringed.

Third Amendment

No Soldier shall, in time of peace be quartered in any house, without the consent of the Owner, nor in time of war, but in a manner to be prescribed by law.

Fourth Amendment

The right of the people to be secure in their persons, houses, papers, and effects, against unreasonable searches and seizures, shall not be violated, and no Warrants shall issue, but upon probable cause, supported by Oath or affirmation, and particularly describing the place to be searched, and the persons or things to be seized.

Fifth Amendment

No person shall be held to answer for a capital, or otherwise infamous crime, unless on a presentment or indictment of a Grand Jury, except in cases arising in the land or naval forces, or in the Militia, when in actual service in time of War or public danger; nor shall any person be subject for the same offence to be twice put in jeopardy of life or limb; nor shall be compelled in any criminal case to be a witness against himself, nor be deprived of life, liberty, or property, without due process of law; nor shall private property be taken for public use, without just compensation.

Sixth Amendment

In all criminal prosecutions, the accused shall enjoy the right to a speedy and public trial, by an impartial jury of the State and district wherein the crime shall have been committed, which district shall have been previously ascertained by law, and to be informed of the nature and cause of the accusation; to be confronted with the witnesses against him; to have compulsory process for obtaining witnesses in his favor, and to have the Assistance of Counsel for his defence.

Seventh Amendment

In Suits at common law, where the value in controversy shall exceed twenty dollars, the right of trial by jury shall be preserved, and no fact tried by a jury, shall be otherwise reexamined in any Court of the United States, than according to the rules of the common law.

Eighth Amendment

Excessive bail shall not be required, nor excessive fines imposed, nor cruel and unusual punishments inflicted.

Ninth Amendment

The enumeration in the Constitution, of certain rights, shall not be construed to deny or disparage others retained by the people.

10th Amendment

The powers not delegated to the United States by the Constitution, nor prohibited by it to the States, are reserved to the States respectively, or to the people.

11th Amendment

The Judicial power of the United States shall not be construed to extend to any suit in law or equity, commenced or prosecuted against one of the United States by Citizens of another State, or by Citizens or Subjects of any Foreign State.

12th Amendment

The Electors shall meet in their respective states and vote by ballot for President and Vice-President, one of whom, at least, shall not be an inhabitant of the same state with themselves; they shall name in their ballots the person voted for as President, and in distinct ballots the person voted for as Vice-President, and they shall make distinct lists of all persons voted for as President, and of all persons voted for as Vice-President, and of the number of votes for each, which lists they shall sign and certify, and transmit sealed to the seat of the government of the United States, directed to the President of the Senate; -- The President of the Senate shall, in the presence of the Senate and House of Representatives, open all the certificates and the votes shall then be counted; -- The person having the greatest number of votes for President, shall be the President, if such number be a majority of the whole number of Electors appointed; and if no person have such majority, then from the persons having the highest numbers not exceeding three on the list of those voted for as President, the House of Representatives shall choose immediately, by ballot, the President. But in choosing the President, the votes shall be taken by states, the representation from each state having one vote; a quorum for this purpose shall consist of a member or members from two-thirds of the states, and a majority of all the states shall be necessary to a choice. And if the House of Representatives shall not choose a President whenever the right of choice shall devolve upon them, before the fourth day of March next following, then the Vice-President shall act as President, as in case of the death or other constitutional disability of the President.-- The person having the greatest number of votes as Vice-President, shall be the Vice-President, if such number be a majority of the whole number of Electors appointed, and if no person have a majority, then from the two highest numbers on the list, the Senate shall choose the Vice-President; a quorum for the purpose shall consist of two-thirds of the whole number of Senators, and a majority of the whole number shall be necessary to a choice. But no person constitutionally ineligible to the office of President shall be eligible to that of Vice-President of the United States.

13th Amendment

Section 1

Neither slavery nor involuntary servitude, except as a punishment for crime whereof the party shall have been duly convicted, shall exist within the United States, or any place subject to their jurisdiction.

Section 2

Congress shall have power to enforce this article by appropriate legislation.

14th Amendment

Section 1

All persons born or naturalized in the United States, and subject to the jurisdiction thereof, are citizens of the United States and of the State wherein they reside. No State shall make or enforce any law which shall abridge the privileges or immunities of citizens of the United States; nor shall any State deprive any person of life, liberty, or property, without due process of law; nor deny to any person within its jurisdiction the equal protection of the laws.

Section 2

Representatives shall be apportioned among the several States according to their respective numbers, counting the whole number of persons in each State, excluding Indians not taxed. But when the right to vote at any election for the choice of electors for President and Vice-President of the United States, Representatives in Congress, the Executive and Judicial officers of a State, or the members of the Legislature thereof, is denied to any of the male inhabitants of such State, being twenty-one years of age, and citizens of the United States, or in any way abridged, except for participation in rebellion, or other crime, the basis of representation therein shall be reduced in the proportion which the number of such male citizens shall bear to the whole number of male citizens twenty-one years of age in such State.

Section 3

No person shall be a Senator or Representative in Congress, or elector of President and Vice-President, or hold any office, civil or military, under the United States, or under any State, who, having previously taken an oath, as a member of Congress, or as an officer of the United States, or as a member of any State legislature, or as an executive or judicial officer of any State, to support the Constitution of the United States, shall have engaged in insurrection or rebellion against the same, or given aid or comfort to the enemies thereof. But Congress may by a vote of two-thirds of each House, remove such disability.

Section 4

The validity of the public debt of the United States, authorized by law, including debts incurred for payment of pensions and bounties for services in suppressing insurrection or rebellion, shall not be questioned. But neither the United States nor any State shall assume or pay any debt or obligation incurred in aid of insurrection or rebellion against the United States, or any claim for the loss or emancipation of any slave; but all such debts, obligations and claims shall be held illegal and void.

Section 5

The Congress shall have the power to enforce, by appropriate legislation, the provisions of this article.

15th Amendment

Section 1

The right of citizens of the United States to vote shall not be denied or abridged by the United States or by any State on account of race, color, or previous condition of servitude.

Section 2

The Congress shall have the power to enforce this article by appropriate legislation.

16th Amendment
The Congress shall have power to lay and collect taxes on incomes, from whatever source derived, without apportionment among the several States, and without regard to any census or enumeration.

17th Amendment

The Senate of the United States shall be composed of two Senators from each State, elected by the people thereof, for six years; and each Senator shall have one vote. The electors in each State shall have the qualifications requisite for electors of the most numerous branch of the State legislatures.

When vacancies happen in the representation of any State in the Senate, the executive authority of such State shall issue writs of election to fill such vacancies: Provided, That the legislature of any State may empower the executive thereof to make temporary appointments until the people fill the vacancies by election as the legislature may direct.

This amendment shall not be so construed as to affect the election or term of any Senator chosen before it becomes valid as part of the Constitution.

18th Amendment

Section 1

After one year from the ratification of this article the manufacture, sale, or transportation of intoxicating liquors within, the importation thereof into, or the exportation thereof from the United States and all territory subject to the jurisdiction thereof for beverage purposes is hereby prohibited.

Section 2

The Congress and the several States shall have concurrent power to enforce this article by appropriate legislation.

Section 3

This article shall be inoperative unless it shall have been ratified as an amendment to the Constitution by the legislatures of the several States, as provided in the Constitution, within seven years from the date of the submission hereof to the States by the Congress.

19th Amendment

The right of citizens of the United States to vote shall not be denied or abridged by the United States or by any State on account of sex.

Congress shall have power to enforce this article by appropriate legislation.

20th Amendment

Section 1

The terms of the President and the Vice President shall end at noon on the 20th day of January, and the terms of Senators and Representatives at noon on the 3d day of January, of the years in which such terms would have ended if this article had not been ratified; and the terms of their successors shall then begin.

Section 2

The Congress shall assemble at least once in every year, and such meeting shall begin at noon on the 3d day of January, unless they shall by law appoint a different day.

Section 3

If, at the time fixed for the beginning of the term of the President, the President elect shall have died, the Vice President elect shall become President. If a President shall not have been chosen before the time fixed for the beginning of his term, or if the President elect shall have failed to qualify, then the Vice President elect shall act as President until a President shall have qualified; and the Congress may by law provide for the case wherein neither a President elect nor a Vice

President shall have qualified, declaring who shall then act as President, or the manner in which one who is to act shall be selected, and such person shall act accordingly until a President or Vice President shall have qualified.

Section 4

The Congress may by law provide for the case of the death of any of the persons from whom the House of Representatives may choose a President whenever the right of choice shall have devolved upon them, and for the case of the death of any of the persons from whom the Senate may choose a Vice President whenever the right of choice shall have devolved upon them.

Section 5

Sections 1 and 2 shall take effect on the 15th day of October following the ratification of this article.

Section 6

This article shall be inoperative unless it shall have been ratified as an amendment to the Constitution by the legislatures of three-fourths of the several States within seven years from the date of its submission.

21st Amendment

Section 1

The eighteenth article of amendment to the Constitution of the United States is hereby repealed.

Section 2

The transportation or importation into any State, Territory, or Possession of the United States for delivery or use therein of intoxicating liquors, in violation of the laws thereof, is hereby prohibited.

Section 3

This article shall be inoperative unless it shall have been ratified as an amendment to the Constitution by conventions in the several States, as provided in the Constitution, within seven years from the date of the submission hereof to the States by the Congress.

22nd Amendment

Section 1

No person shall be elected to the office of the President more than twice, and no person who has held the office of President, or acted as President, for more than two years of a term to which some other person was elected President shall be elected to the office of President more than once. But this Article shall not apply to any person holding the office of President when this Article was proposed by Congress, and shall not prevent any person who may be holding the office of President, or acting as President, during the term within which this Article becomes operative from holding the office of President or acting as President during the remainder of such term.

Section 2

This article shall be inoperative unless it shall have been ratified as an amendment to the Constitution by the legislatures of three-fourths of the several States within seven years from the date of its submission to the States by the Congress.

23rd Amendment

Section 1

The District constituting the seat of Government of the United States shall appoint in such manner as Congress may direct:

A number of electors of President and Vice President equal to the whole number of Senators and Representatives in Congress to which the District would be entitled if it were a State, but in no event more than the least populous State; they shall be in addition to those appointed by the States, but they shall be considered, for the purposes of the election of President and Vice President, to be electors appointed by a State; and they shall meet in the District and perform such duties as provided by the twelfth article of amendment.

Section 2

The Congress shall have power to enforce this article by appropriate legislation.

24th Amendment

Section 1

The right of citizens of the United States to vote in any primary or other election for President or Vice President, for electors for President or Vice President, or for Senator or Representative in Congress, shall not be denied or abridged by the United States or any State by reason of failure to pay poll tax or other tax.

Section 2

The Congress shall have power to enforce this article by appropriate legislation.

25th Amendment

Section 1

In case of the removal of the President from office or of his death or resignation, the Vice President shall become President.

Section 2

Whenever there is a vacancy in the office of the Vice President, the President shall nominate a Vice President who shall take office upon confirmation by a majority vote of both Houses of Congress.

Section 3

Whenever the President transmits to the President pro tempore of the Senate and the Speaker of the House of Representatives his written declaration that he is unable to discharge the powers and duties of his office, and until he transmits to them a written declaration to the contrary, such powers and duties shall be discharged by the Vice President as Acting President.

Section 4

Whenever the Vice President and a majority of either the principal officers of the executive departments or of such other body as Congress may by law provide, transmit to the President pro tempore of the Senate and the Speaker of the House of Representatives their written declaration that the President is unable to discharge the powers and duties of his office, the Vice President shall immediately assume the powers and duties of the office as Acting President.

Thereafter, when the President transmits to the President pro tempore of the Senate and the Speaker of the House of Representatives his written declaration that no inability exists, he shall resume the powers and duties of his office unless the Vice President and a majority of either the principal officers of the executive department or of such other body as Congress may by law provide, transmit within four days to the President pro tempore of the Senate and the Speaker of the House of Representatives their written declaration that the President is unable to discharge the powers and duties of his office. Thereupon Congress shall decide the issue, assembling within forty-eight hours for that purpose if not in session. If the Congress, within twenty-one days after receipt of the latter written declaration, or, if Congress is not in session, within twenty-one days after Congress is required to assemble, determines by two-thirds vote of both Houses that the President is unable to discharge the powers and duties of his office, the Vice

President shall continue to discharge the same as Acting President; otherwise, the President shall resume the powers and duties of his office.

26th Amendment

Section 1

The right of citizens of the United States, who are eighteen years of age or older, to vote shall not be denied or abridged by the United States or by any State on account of age.

Section 2

The Congress shall have power to enforce this article by appropriate legislation.

27th Amendment

No law, varying the compensation for the services of the Senators and Representatives, shall take effect, until an election of representatives shall have intervened.

APPENDIX 2 - ARTICLES OF CONFEDERATION

To all to whom these Presents shall come, we, the undersigned Delegates of the States affixed to our Names send greeting. Whereas the Delegates of the United States of America in Congress assembled did on the fifteenth day of November in the year of our Lord One Thousand Seven Hundred and Seventy seven, and in the Second Year of the Independence of America agree to certain articles of Confederation and perpetual Union between the States of Newhampshire, Massachusetts-bay, Rhodeisland and Providence Plantations, Connecticut, New York, New Jersey, Pennsylvania, Delaware, Maryland, Virginia, North Carolina, South Carolina, and Georgia in the Words following, viz. "Articles of Confederation and perpetual Union between the States of Newhampshire, Massachusetts-bay, Rhodeisland and Providence Plantations, Connecticut, New York, New Jersey, Pennsylvania, Delaware, Maryland, Virginia, North Carolina, South Carolina, and Georgia.

Article I.

The Stile of this confederacy shall be, "The United States of America."

Article II.

Each state retains its sovereignty, freedom and independence, and every Power, Jurisdiction and right, which is not by this confederation expressly delegated to the united states, in Congress assembled.

Article III.

The said states hereby severally enter into a firm league of friendship with each other, for their common defence, the security of their Liberties, and their mutual and general welfare, binding themselves to assist each other, against all force offered to, or attacks made upon them, or any of them, on account of religion, sovereignty, trade, or any other pretence whatever.

Article IV.

The better to secure and perpetuate mutual friendship and intercourse among the people of the different states in this union, the free inhabitants of each of these states, paupers, vagabonds and fugitives from Justice excepted, shall be entitled to all privileges and immunities of free citizens in the several states; and the people of each state shall have free ingress and regress to and from any other state, and shall enjoy therein all the privileges of trade and commerce, subject to the same duties, impositions and restrictions as the inhabitants thereof respectively, provided that such restrictions shall not extend so far as to prevent the removal of property imported into any state, to any other State of which the Owner is an inhabitant; provided also that no imposition, duties or restriction shall be laid by any state, on the property of the united states, or either of them.

If any Person guilty of, or charged with, treason, felony, or other high misdemeanor in any state, shall flee from Justice, and be found in any of the united states, he shall upon demand of the Governor or executive power of the state from which he fled, be delivered up, and removed to the state having jurisdiction of his offense.

Full faith and credit shall be given in each of these states to the records, acts and judicial proceedings of the courts and magistrates of every other state.

Article V.

For the more convenient management of the general interests of the united states, delegates shall be annually appointed in such manner as the legislature of each state shall direct, to meet in Congress on the first Monday in November, in every year, with a power reserved to each state to recall its delegates, or any of them, at any time within the year, and to send others in their stead, for the remainder of the Year.

No State shall be represented in Congress by less than two, nor by more than seven Members; and no person shall be capable of being delegate for more than three years, in any term of six years; nor shall any person, being a delegate, be capable of holding any office under the united states, for which he, or another for his benefit receives any salary, fees or emolument of any kind.

Each State shall maintain its own delegates in a meeting of the states, and while they act as members of the committee of the states.

In determining questions in the united states, in Congress assembled, each state shall have one vote.

Freedom of speech and debate in Congress shall not be impeached or questioned in any Court, or place out of Congress, and the members of congress shall be protected in their persons from arrests and imprisonments, during the time of their going to and from, and attendance on congress, except for treason, felony, or breach of the peace.

Article VI.

No State, without the Consent of the united states, in congress assembled, shall send any embassy to, or receive any embassy from, or enter into any conferrence, agreement, alliance, or treaty, with any King prince or state; nor shall any person holding any office of profit or trust under the united states, or any of them, accept of any present, emolument, office, or title of any kind whatever, from any king, prince, or foreign state; nor shall the united states, in congress assembled, or any of them, grant any title of nobility.

No two or more states shall enter into any treaty, confederation, or alliance whatever between them, without the consent of the united states, in congress assembled, specifying accurately the purposes for which the same is to be entered into, and how long it shall continue.

No State shall lay any imposts or duties, which may interfere with any stipulations in treaties, entered into by the united states in congress assembled, with any king, prince, or State, in pursuance of any treaties already proposed by congress, to the courts of France and Spain.

No vessels of war shall be kept up in time of peace, by any state, except such number only, as shall be deemed necessary by the united states, in congress assembled, for the defence of such state, or its trade; nor shall any body of forces be kept up, by any state, in time of peace, except such number only as, in the judgment of the united states, in congress assembled, shall be deemed requisite to garrison the forts necessary for the defence of such state; but every state shall always keep up a well regulated and disciplined militia, sufficiently armed and accoutred, and shall provide and constantly have ready for use, in public stores, a due number of field pieces and tents, and a proper quantity of arms, ammunition, and camp equipage.

No State shall engage in any war without the consent of the united states in congress assembled, unless such State be actually invaded by enemies, or shall have received certain advice of a resolution being formed by some nation of Indians to invade such State, and the danger is so imminent as not to admit of a delay till the united states in congress assembled, can be consulted: nor shall any state grant commissions to any ships or vessels of war, nor letters of marque or reprisal, except it be after a declaration of war by the united states in congress assembled, and then only against the kingdom or State, and the subjects thereof, against which war has been so declared, and under such regulations as shall be established by the united states in congress assembled, unless such state be infested by pirates, in which case vessels of war may be fitted out for that occasion, and kept so long as the danger shall continue, or until the united states in congress assembled shall determine otherwise.

Article VII.

When land forces are raised by any state, for the common defence, all officers of or under the rank of colonel, shall be appointed by the legislature of each state respectively by whom such forces shall be raised, or in such manner as such state shall direct, and all vacancies shall be filled up by the state which first made appointment.

Article VIII.

All charges of war, and all other expenses that shall be incurred for the common defence or general welfare, and allowed by the united states in congress assembled, shall be defrayed out of a common treasury, which shall be supplied by the several states, in proportion to the value of all land within each state, granted to or surveyed for any

Person, as such land and the buildings and improvements thereon shall be estimated, according to such mode as the united states, in congress assembled, shall, from time to time, direct and appoint. The taxes for paying that proportion shall be laid and levied by the authority and direction of the legislatures of the several states within the time agreed upon by the united states in congress assembled.

Article IX.

The united states, in congress assembled, shall have the sole and exclusive right and power of determining on peace and war, except in the cases mentioned in the sixth article - of sending and receiving ambassadors - entering into treaties and alliances, provided that no treaty of commerce shall be made, whereby the legislative power of the respective states shall be restrained from imposing such imposts and duties on foreigners, as their own people are subjected to, or from prohibiting the exportation or importation of any species of goods or commodities whatsoever - of establishing rules for deciding, in all cases, what captures on land or water shall be legal, and in what manner prizes taken by land or naval forces in the service of the united states, shall be divided or appropriated - of granting letters of marque and reprisal in times of peace - appointing courts for the trial of piracies and felonies committed on the high seas; and establishing courts; for receiving and determining finally appeals in all cases of captures; provided that no member of congress shall be appointed a judge of any of the said courts.

The united states, in congress assembled, shall also be the last resort on appeal, in all disputes and differences now subsisting, or that hereafter may arise between two or more states concerning boundary, jurisdiction, or any other cause whatever; which authority shall always be exercised in the manner following. Whenever the legislative or executive authority, or lawful agent of any state in controversy with another, shall present a petition to congress, stating the matter in question, and praying for a hearing, notice thereof shall be given, by order of congress, to the legislative or executive authority of the other state in controversy, and a day assigned for the appearance of the parties by their lawful agents, who shall then be directed to appoint, by joint consent, commissioners or judges to constitute a court for hearing and determining the matter in question: but if they cannot agree, congress shall name three persons out of each of the united states, and from the list of such persons each party shall alternately strike out one, the petitioners beginning, until the number shall be reduced to thirteen; and from that number not less than seven, nor more than nine names, as congress shall direct, shall, in the presence of congress, be drawn out by lot, and the persons whose names shall be so drawn, or any five of them, shall be commissioners or judges, to hear and finally determine the controversy, so always as a major part of the judges, who shall hear the cause, shall agree in the determination: and if either party shall neglect to attend at the day appointed, without showing reasons which congress shall judge sufficient, or being present, shall refuse to strike, the congress shall proceed to nominate three persons out of each State, and the secretary of congress shall strike in behalf of such party absent or refusing; and the judgment and sentence of the court, to be appointed in the manner before prescribed, shall be final and conclusive; and if any of the parties shall refuse to submit to the authority of such court, or to appear or defend their claim or cause, the court shall nevertheless proceed to pronounce sentence, or judgment, which shall in like manner be final and decisive; the judgment or sentence and other proceedings being in either case transmitted to congress, and lodged among the acts of congress, for the security of the parties concerned: provided that every commissioner, before he sits in judgment, shall take an oath to be administered by one of the judges of the supreme or superior court of the State where the cause shall be tried, "well and truly to hear and determine the matter in question, according to the best of his judgment, without favor, affection, or hope of reward: "provided, also, that no State shall be deprived of territory for the benefit of the united states.

All controversies concerning the private right of soil claimed under different grants of two or more states, whose jurisdictions as they may respect such lands, and the states which passed such grants are adjusted, the said grants or either of them being at the same time claimed to have originated antecedent to such settlement of jurisdiction, shall, on the petition of either party to the congress of the united states, be finally determined, as near as may be, in the same manner as is before prescribed for deciding disputes respecting territorial jurisdiction between different states.

The united states, in congress assembled, shall also have the sole and exclusive right and power of regulating the alloy and value of coin struck by their own authority, or by that of the respective states -

fixing the standard of weights and measures throughout the united states - regulating the trade and managing all affairs with the Indians, not members of any of the states; provided that the legislative right of any state, within its own limits, be not infringed or violated - establishing and regulating post-offices from one state to another, throughout all the united states, and exacting such postage on the papers passing through the same, as may be requisite to defray the expenses of the said office - appointing all officers of the land forces in the service of the united states, excepting regimental officers - appointing all the officers of the naval forces, and commissioning all officers whatever in the service of the united states; making rules for the government and regulation of the said land and naval forces, and directing their operations.

The united states, in congress assembled, shall have authority to appoint a committee, to sit in the recess of congress, to be denominated, "A Committee of the States," and to consist of one delegate from each State; and to appoint such other committees and civil officers as may be necessary for managing the general affairs of the united states under their direction - to appoint one of their number to preside; provided that no person be allowed to serve in the office of president more than one year in any term of three years; to ascertain the necessary sums of money to be raised for the service of the united states, and to appropriate and apply the same for defraying the public expenses; to borrow money or emit bills on the credit of the united states, transmitting every half year to the respective states an account of the sums of money so borrowed or emitted, - to build and equip a navy - to agree upon the number of land forces, and to make requisitions from each state for its quota, in proportion to the number of white inhabitants in such state, which requisition shall be binding; and thereupon the legislature of each state shall appoint the regimental officers, raise the men, and clothe, arm, and equip them, in a soldier-like manner, at the expense of the united states; and the officers and men so clothed, armed, and equipped, shall march to the place appointed, and within the time agreed on by the united states, in congress assembled; but if the united states, in congress assembled, shall, on consideration of circumstances, judge proper that any state should not raise men, or should raise a smaller number than its quota, and that any other state should raise a greater number of men than the quota thereof, such extra number shall be raised, officered, clothed, armed, and equipped in the same manner as the quota of such state, unless the legislature of such state shall judge that such extra number cannot be safely spared out of the same, in which case they shall raise, officer, clothe, arm, and equip, as many of such extra number as they judge can be safely spared. And the officers and men so clothed, armed, and equipped, shall march to the place appointed, and within the time agreed on by the united states in congress assembled.

The united states, in congress assembled, shall never engage in a war, nor grant letters of marque and reprisal in time of peace, nor enter into any treaties or alliances, nor coin money, nor regulate the value thereof nor ascertain the sums and expenses necessary for the defence and welfare of the united states, or any of them, nor emit bills, nor borrow money on the credit of the united states, nor appropriate money, nor agree upon the number of vessels of war to be built or purchased, or the number of land or sea forces to be raised, nor appoint a commander in chief of the army or navy, unless nine states assent to the same, nor shall a question on any other point, except for adjourning from day to day, be determined, unless by the votes of a majority of the united states in congress assembled.

The congress of the united states shall have power to adjourn to any time within the year, and to any place within the united states, so that no period of adjournment be for a longer duration than the space of six Months, and shall publish the Journal of their proceedings monthly, except such parts thereof relating to treaties, alliances, or military operations, as in their judgment require secrecy; and the yeas and nays of the delegates of each State, on any question, shall be entered on the Journal, when it is desired by any delegate; and the delegates of a State, or any of them, at his or their request, shall be furnished with a transcript of the said Journal, except such parts as are above excepted, to lay before the legislatures of the several states.

Article X.

The committee of the states, or any nine of them, shall be authorized to execute, in the recess of congress, such of the powers of congress as the united states, in congress assembled, by the consent of nine states, shall, from time to time, think expedient to vest them with; provided that no power be delegated to the said committee, for the exercise of which, by the articles of confederation, the voice of nine states, in the congress of the united states assembled, is requisite.

Article XI.

Canada acceding to this confederation, and joining in the measures of the United States, shall be admitted into, and entitled to all the advantages of this union: but no other colony shall be admitted into the same, unless such admission be agreed to by nine states.

Article XII.

All bills of credit emitted, monies borrowed, and debts contracted by or under the authority of congress, before the assembling of the united states, in pursuance of the present confederation, shall be deemed and considered as a charge against the united States, for payment and satisfaction whereof the said united states and the public faith are hereby solemnly pledged.

Article XIII.

Every State shall abide by the determinations of the united states, in congress assembled, on all questions which by this confederation are submitted to them. And the Articles of this confederation shall be inviolably observed by every state, and the union shall be perpetual; nor shall any alteration at any time hereafter be made in any of them, unless such alteration be agreed to in a congress of the united states, and be afterwards con-firmed by the legislatures of every state.

And Whereas it hath pleased the Great Governor of the World to incline the hearts of the legislatures we respectively represent in congress, to approve of, and to authorize us to ratify the said articles of confederation and perpetual union, Know Ye, that we, the undersigned delegates, by virtue of the power and authority to us given for that purpose, do, by these presents, in the name and in behalf of our respective constituents, fully and entirely ratify and confirm each and every of the said articles of confederation and perpetual union, and all and singular the matters and things therein contained. And we do further solemnly plight and engage the faith of our respective constituents, that they shall abide by the determinations of the united states in congress assembled, on all questions, which by the said confederation are submitted to them. And that the articles thereof shall be inviolably observed by the states we respectively represent, and that the union shall be perpetual. In Witness whereof, we have hereunto set our hands, in Congress. Done at Philadelphia, in the State of Pennsylvania, the ninth Day of July, in the Year of our Lord one Thousand seven Hundred and Seventy eight, and in the third year of the Independence of America.

APPENDIX 3 - SIMULATED CONVENTION RULES

Rule 1. Questions not governed by these rules shall be governed by the latest published edition of Mason's Manual of Legislative Procedure, except where the rule in that manual can be applied only to a state legislature rather than a convention; in which case the matter shall be determined by parliamentary common law.[1]

Rule 2. The administrator of this simulated convention is Citizens for Self-Governance, an association with its principal office at 106 East Street, Suite 900, Austin, TX 78701.

Rule 3. Officers
- The officers of the convention shall consist of a president and vice president, who shall be elected from among the commissioners; and a secretary, sergeant-at-arms, and parliamentarian, who shall be designated by the administrator from among persons not commissioners.[2] Election for president shall be by a majority of states. The person who receives the second-highest vote total in the tally in which the winning candidate for president receives a majority shall become vice president.[3] The convention officers shall discharge duties usually to such officers pursuant to Mason's Manual and parliamentary common law, subject to alteration by the convention. All officers shall be on oath to carry out their obligations faithfully and in accordance with lawful authority.
- The temporary convention president shall be appointed from among the commissioners from the state that was the first to adopt the CoS form application—that is to say, Georgia. The temporary president shall be selected by a majority vote of that state's delegation. The temporary president's sole duty shall be

---

1 Seventy of the 99 state legislative chambers currently use Mason's Manual as their source of default rules. Additional rules for selecting this source are explained in COMPENDIUM, §3.14.4. The parliamentary common law is the American common law of organizational procedures built up over several centuries. It has that name because it was derived originally from procedures in the British Parliament.

2 The CoS Model Convention Rules provide for all these officers to be elected. They also provide for an assistant parliamentarian. The version above reflects the time constraints of a two-day simulation.

3 In an actual convention the president and vice-president would be elected separately by majority votes of the states. This rule was adapted to save time.

to preside over the election of the convention president and vice-president. He or she shall be ineligible to be the permanent president or permanent vice-president.

- In addition to such other duties as shall be prescribed by the convention or by the presiding officer, the secretary shall prepare and provide to each commissioner at the opening or beginning of business on each day a calendar or agenda of business scheduled for that day.

Rule 4. The sergeant-at-arms is empowered, under direction of the presiding officer to secure the good order of the house. Orders issued by the president to the sergeant-of-arms shall be appealable, as in the case of other rulings of the chair.

Rule 5. The members of this convention are the delegations from each of the several states. All votes shall be taken by states, with each state having one vote. In roll call votes, states shall declare their votes in alphabetical order.[4]

Rule 6. Irrespective of how many commissioners a state includes within its delegation, no more than five commissioners from any one state shall be on the floor at the same time.[5] On every vote, the state's vote shall be announced by the chair of the state delegation or his or her designee. Every delegation shall canvass each commissioner on each vote in a manner to be prescribed by the delegation. Each state delegation's vote shall be determined in accordance with a plurality vote of that delegation.[6]

---

4 The traditional order was for states to vote from northeast to southwest, but the current configuration of the country makes that difficult, and the alphabetical system is more familiar to modern Americans.
5 This rule addresses the unfair and potentially unruly situation arising at the 1850 Nashville Convention, where Tennessee, although having only one vote, sent 100 commissioners, more than all other states combined. The COMPENDIUM recommends a maximum of five, which is justified by the fact that this convention will include many more states than earlier conventions. The rules take account of the fact that some states may wish to appoint alternate commissioners.
6 In the CoS Model Convention Rules, the commissioning state determines how each delegation casts its vote. Because there are no commissioning states for the simulation, this rule designates a procedure. The required vote is a plurality rather than a majority so as to disregard absences and abstentions.

Rule 7. Before the opening of business each day every commissioner shall sign a sheet provided by the secretary indicating that commissioner's attendance and the state he or she is representing. A quorum to do business shall consist of the commissioners empowered to cast the votes of more than half of the state delegations accredited to the convention, and all questions shall be decided by the greater number of delegations present; but in absence of a quorum a majority of delegations present may recess for the day. [7]

Rule 8. The order of business shall be as follows:[8]
- call to order
- announcement by secretary of whether a quorum is present
- invocation
- pledge of allegiance
- consideration of the minutes of the previous day
- reports of committees
- unfinished business
- new business
- announcement of committee meetings, and
- recess for the day (adjournment).[9]

Rule 9. Every commissioner rising to speak shall address the presiding officer; and while he or she shall be speaking no one shall pass between them or read any written matter not immediately germane to the question under consideration.[10]

---

7 This rule is based on the rules of the 1861 Washington Convention. COMPENDIUM §3.14.3. The term "day to day" from the original rules has been deleted, since this is only a two-day simulation. The word "recess" to describe an adjournment from day-to-day is used in Mason's Manual.
8 This is the order in Mason's Manual, as modified for the fact that this is a convention not a legislative body, COMPENDIUM §3.14.5, and simplified for the simulation. The pledge of allegiance has been added in this version.
9 The word "recess" to describe an adjournment from day-to-day is used in Mason's Manual.
10 This is based on the rules prevailing both at the 1787 Philadelphia Convention and the 1861 Washington Convention, although modified to take account of modern technology. COMPENDIUM § 3.14.5.

Rule 10. Of two commissioners rising to speak at the same time, the presiding officer shall name the one who shall first be heard.

Rule 11. A commissioner shall not speak more often than twice without special leave upon the same question; and not a second time before every other who had been silent but shall choose to speak on the subject shall have been heard.

Rule 12. No commissioner shall, without leave of the convention, speak more than five minutes at any one time.[11]

Rule 13. A motion made and seconded shall be repeated; and if written, as it shall be when any commissioner shall so require, shall be projected on a common screen. No motion, other than a procedural motion, shall be in order unless within the scope of the subject matter of the form application of the Citizens for Self-Governance Convention of States project.

Rule 14. A motion may be withdrawn at any time before the vote upon it shall have been declared.[12]

Rule 15. When a debate shall arise upon a question, no motion, other than to amend the question, to commit it, or to postpone the debate, shall be received.[13]

Rule 16. A question that consists of one or more propositions shall, at the request of any commissioner, be divided and put separately as to each proposition.[14]

---

11 Added to reflect modern conditions, COMPENDIUM §3.14.5, but shortened from 10 minutes in the CoS Model Convention Rules.
12 Based on the Washington Convention rules.
13 Based on the Washington Convention rules.
14 Based on a rule of the Washington Convention. The language has been updated. The CoS Model Convention Rules include a provision that "No substantive question or committee recommendation shall be decided the day on which it is introduced or first debated, if any five states request that the decision be postponed to another day." There is another provision that "A motion to reconsider a matter that has been determined by a majority may be made, with leave unanimously given, on the same day on which the vote passed; but otherwise not without one day's previous notice; in which last case, if the convention agree to the reconsideration, the convention or, by the convention's leave, the president shall assign a future day for the purpose." Those are omitted here as impractical in a two-day simulation.

Rule 17. A commissioner may be called to order by another commissioner, as well as by the presiding officer, and may be allowed to explain any conduct or expressions supposed to be reprehensible.[15]

Rule 18. All questions of order shall be decided by the presiding officer, subject to appeal to the convention, but without debate.[16]

Rule 19. Upon a question to recess for the day, which may be made at any time, if it be seconded, the question shall be put without debate.[17]

Rule 20. No commissioner shall be absent from the convention, so as to interrupt the representation of his or her state, without leave.[18]

Rule 21. Committees—generally applicable provisions
1. The administrator shall perform the normal functions of committees on rules, credentials, and administration.[19] The standing committees in this simulated convention are (a) fiscal restraints, (b) federal legislative and executive jurisdiction, and (c) term limits/federal judicial jurisdiction.[20] The membership of these committees shall be selected by the method designated in Rule 22.
2. The convention may create ad hoc committees. Their members shall be appointed by the presiding officer at the time, unless the convention shall prescribe another method. Each committee may create subcommittees for issues germane to the committee's assigned task.

---

15 COMPENDIUM §3.14.5.
16 A proposed rule of the Washington Convention would have dispensed with the right of appeal, but the delegates rejected that provision. COMPENDIUM §3.14.5.17 Based on a rule of the Washington Convention. COMPENDIUM §3.14.5.
17 Based on a rule of the Washington Convention. COMPENDIUM §3.14.5.
18 Based on a rule of the Washington Convention, with updated language. COMPENDIUM §3.14.5.
19 The CoS Model Convention Rules provide for convention-elected committees to serve these purposes.
20 The subjects mentioned in this rule are those contained in the CoS legislative application. In the CoS Model Convention Rules, one committee has responsibility for all issues of federal jurisdiction. For this simulation, federal judicial jurisdiction has been moved to the term limits committee.

Committees and subcommittees shall not sit while the convention shall be sitting, without leave of the convention.[21]

Rule 22. Committees on fiscal restraints, federal legislative and executive jurisdiction, and term limits/federal judicial jurisdiction. [22]

- The fiscal restraints committee, federal legislative and executive jurisdiction committee, and the term limits/judicial jurisdiction committee each has exclusive responsibility for developing proposals within the corresponding subject matter of the CoS form application.
- Each of these three committees shall consist of one commissioner from each state delegation, selected as determined by such delegation; provided however, that no person shall serve on more than one of these three committees.
- Any proposal approved by a subcommittee of any of these three committees shall be referred to its committee chairman, who shall schedule it for expedited hearing. Approval shall be by a simple majority of committee members present and voting.
- Each of these three committees shall be entitled to present not more than three proposed amendments for debate and vote on the floor of the convention. The presiding officer of the convention shall have no authority to refuse to schedule debate or a vote on any such proposal, and no formal rule shall be required to schedule any such proposal for debate or a vote. No motion to adjourn sine die shall be in order so long as any such proposal remains without a convention vote to pass, reject, or table.

---

21 Based on a rule of the Washington Convention and modern legislative practice. COMPENDIUM §3.14.5.
22 This rule is a simplified version of the comparable provision in the CoS Model Convention Rules.

APPENDIX 4 – Balanced Budget Amendment Task Force
RULES CONVENTION RESOLUTION 1

Resolution creating rules of procedure for a future convention to propose a balanced budget amendment to the Constitution of the United States convened pursuant to Article V of the Constitution.

PREAMBLE

Pursuant to Article V of the United States Constitution, we the delegates of the several sovereign States, grateful to Almighty God, do assemble in this Convention of the States, called by Congress, for the sole purpose of proposing an amendment to the Constitution.

ARTICLE 1 – Subject of the Convention

1.1 Convention Limited Authority
This Convention is convened under the authority reserved to the state legislatures of the several States by Article V of the Constitution of the United States. The only participants at this Convention are the several States represented by delegations duly selected in such manner as their respective legislatures have determined. The Convention derives its authority from the applications adopted by at least two-thirds of the legislatures of the several States, and its authority is thereby limited to the subject of proposing an amendment to the Constitution of the United States regarding balancing the federal budget as specified in applications from at least two-thirds of the States. This Convention and these delegates have no authority to propose an amendment or amendments on any other subject.

1.2 Temporary Rules
For the purposes of organizing the Convention, all Articles herein shall be adopted by a majority of the States voting, one vote per State, to serve as temporary rules for the Convention save for any Article which requires more than a simple majority shall require, by division, an equal majority of votes by the Convention. The Temporary Rules shall remain in effect until the Rules Committee submits amendments to these rules which are subsequently

approved by the Convention in the same manner as the Temporary Rules were approved.

1.3 Initial Quorum
The initial quorum for the Convention shall be a majority of the several States whose delegate or delegates are physically present at the time of the initial roll call of the Convention.

1.4 Prohibition on Amending or Suspending
Article 1 shall not be amended or suspended by the Convention.

ARTICLE 2 - Officers of the Convention

2.1 List and Duties of Officers

2.1.1 Temporary President
A temporary President shall be an individual selected by the State delegation from the host State to preside and not necessarily a member of the delegation.
Upon the initial assemblage of the Convention, the temporary President shall call the roll of the States, at which time the States shall present their credentials to the temporary President and name all delegates present.

2.1.2 Permanent Officers
The officers of the Convention shall be a President, a Vice President, a Secretary, a Sergeant-at-Arms, and a Parliamentarian. The President and Vice President shall be a member of a State delegation and elected by a simple majority vote of the States voting subject to Article 2.2. The Sergeant-at-Arms, the Parliamentarian and the Secretary shall be appointed by the President with the consent of the Convention, and shall not be a member of a delegation of a State. No more than one elected officer shall be from the same State.

2.1.2.1 Duties of the President

2.1.2.1.1 Calling the Convention to Order
The President or presiding officer shall take the chair each day at the hour to which the Convention shall

convene and shall call the Convention to order and, except in the absence of a quorum as prescribed by these rules, shall proceed to business in the manner prescribed by these rules.

2.1.2.1.2 Duty to Preserve Order and Decorum

The President or presiding officer shall preserve order and decorum, and during debate, shall confine delegations and individual delegates to the question under discussion and shall have general control of the Convention chamber, unless otherwise ordered by the Convention, and in cases of disturbance or disorderly conduct on the floor or in the public areas outside the bar of the Convention, shall have the power to order the same cleared of any parties involved in such a disturbance or disorderly conduct.

2.1.2.1.3 Authority to Enforce Rules

The President or presiding officer may rule out of order, or discipline, any state or delegate for violating provisions of the rules of the Convention. Disciplinary action shall not inhibit the right of a state to cast a vote in the Convention or any committee of the Convention.

2.1.2.1.4 Points of Order

All questions of order shall be decided by the President or presiding officer, subject to appeal to the Convention. On every appeal, the President or presiding officer shall have the right to assign the reason for the decision. In case of such appeal, no State shall speak more than once. All questions and points of order shall be noted by the Secretary with the decision thereof.

2.1.2.1.5 Committee Membership

The President shall be an ex-officio member of all committees of the Convention but shall not be a voting member of any save for the Credentials Committee.

2.1.2.2 Duties of the Vice President

2.1.2.2.1 Absence of the President

In the event of the temporary absence or inability to preside by the President, the Vice-President shall preside over the Convention in the same manner as the President.

2.1.2.2.2 Convention Manager

The Vice President shall serve as the manager of the Convention with the duties to provide necessary facilities, staff, audio visual equipment, and document reproduction at the direction of the Convention and the committees. The Vice President may create a committee to advise the Vice President on these matters.

2.1.2.3 Duties of the Secretary

2.1.2.3.1 General Duties of the Secretary

The Secretary shall be custodian of the records of the Convention and shall perform the customary duties of clerks or secretaries of deliberative assemblies and such other duties as shall be ordered by the Convention.

2.1.2.3.2 Journal Record of Proceedings

The Secretary shall keep a journal of the proceedings of the Convention and shall publish an electronic copy from the proceedings of the previous day. The attested "Journal of Proceedings" provided for in 2.1.2.3.6 below shall be the official legal record of the Convention.

2.1.2.3.3 Verbatim Record of Proceedings

The Secretary shall cause to be produced a verbatim record of the daily floor sessions of the Convention and shall likewise cause verbatim records to be produced of each committee meeting convened in the course of the Convention. The verbatim records required herein shall be published in electronic form and be made available to the public via the Convention's website and any other means as soon as they are reasonably available.

2.1.2.3.4 Numbering of Proposals
The Secretary shall give to every proposal when introduced a number, and the numbers shall be in sequential order.

2.1.2.3.5 Preparation of Calendar, Reports, and Amendments
The Secretary shall prepare and provide to each delegate each day a calendar of the business of the Convention, as provided by these rules, and shall arrange and publish all committee reports and all amendments offered to pending amendments.

2.1.2.3.6 Preservation of Records
As soon as possible after the final adjournment of the Convention, the Secretary shall prepare a "Journal of Proceedings" of the Convention, which shall be attested to by the President and the Vice President. The Secretary shall cause the journal to be both physically and electronically published in full. The Secretary shall cause the audio and video records of the Convention to be compiled and preserved and shall file the journal and all audio and video records with the Archivist of the United States for keeping in the manner provided by law for the records, books, video and audio records, documents, and other papers of the Convention. Likewise, the same records shall be filed with the Library of Congress, and with the several States in a manner directed by the Convention. The Secretary shall additionally send copies of all such records to the Speaker of the United States House of Representatives, the President of the United States Senate, the Clerk of the United States House of Representatives and the Secretary of the United States Senate.

2.1.2.3.7 Necessary Deputies and Staff
The Secretary may secure necessary staff and assign deputies to fulfill such duties as may arise in the course of the Convention.

2.1.2.3.8 Vote Tally
Whenever an issue is considered for a vote of the States, the Secretary (or Clerk) shall call the roll, note how each State voted (Aye, Nay, Divided, or Pass), tally the votes, and present the results to the President.

2.1.2.4 Duties of the Parliamentarian

2.1.2.4.1 Qualifications
The Chief Parliamentarian and any Assistant Parliamentarians shall be a current or former member of the Mason's Manual Commission. The Chief Parliamentarian shall have previously served as the Chief or Head Parliamentarian of a state legislative body. A Parliamentarian shall not be a delegate. Each committee shall be assigned an Assistant Parliamentarian upon request to the Chief Parliamentarian, who will make such assignment.

2.1.2.4.2 Duties
Upon request, the Parliamentarian shall advise the presiding officer of the Convention or a committee regarding questions of parliamentary procedure or the rules of the Convention.

2.1.2.5 Duties of the Sergeant-at-Arms

2.1.2.5.1 Convention
Subject to the direction of the President or presiding officer, the Sergeant-at-Arms shall enforce the rules of the Convention. The Sergeant-at-Arms shall be charged with enforcing the rules as to admission on the Convention floor, only delegates and designated staff are permitted to be on the Convention floor without leave of the body.

2.1.2.5.2 Committees
Subject to the direction of the committee Chair, the Sergeant-at-Arms shall enforce the rules to admission of the committee.

2.1.2.5.3 Deputies

The Sergeant-at-Arms, under the direction of the Secretary may arrange for deputies to fulfill the duties of the Sergeant-at-Arms.

2.1.3 Vacancy of an Officer

In the event of a vacancy of the President, the Vice President shall temporarily rise to President and conduct an election for a new permanent President. After the election of the President, the temporary President shall return to the position of Vice President unless elected President, and the President shall preside. In the event of a vacancy of any other Office, the Office shall be filled in the same manner as prescribed in Article 2.2 with the highest-ranking officer presiding over the election.

2.2 Election of the Officers

The election of the President and Vice President shall be conducted by the temporary President. Nominations shall be made from the floor. Voting shall be by roll call vote by the States with one vote per State. Voting shall continue with successive rounds, with the individual receiving the fewest votes removed from consideration, until an individual receives a simple majority of the States attending and voting. After the election of the officers, the temporary President shall retire and the President shall preside.

ARTICLE 3 – Quorums and Voting

3.1 Quorum

Subject to Article 1.3, a quorum for all committee or voting sessions of the Convention shall be a majority of the States present and for all committee meetings shall be a majority of the members present. At least one delegate from a State who is physically present at a quorum call during a committee or voting session of the Convention shall result in the presence of that State for the purposes of establishing or determining the presence of a quorum.

3.2 Voting

3.2.1 Voting by States

All voting at the Convention or in a committee shall be by State with each State having one vote, without apportionment or division. Each State shall determine the internal voting and quorum rules for casting the vote of its delegation.

3.2.2 Majority Vote

A majority vote of the quorum shall prevail on all issues before the Convention and in all committees, save for any vote to create a rule which requires a majority greater than a simple majority, which shall then require an equal majority to prevail.

3.2.3 Proposing an Amendment for Ratification

An affirmative vote of a majority of States attending and voting shall be necessary to propose an amendment for ratification by the several States.

ARTICLE 4 – Committees

4.1 Rules Committee

After the initial session of the Convention, the Rules Committee shall organize.

4.1.1 Purpose of the Committee

The committee shall review the rules of the Convention and make recommendations to the Convention regarding the addition of committees, the duties of the Officers, and procedures.

4.1.2 Seating and Participation

One delegate has the right to occupy the seat of the State and speak and vote on behalf of the State and the balance of the delegation may be seated in the same location, space provided, and the State may substitute the delegate in the seat of the State at its discretion.

4.1.3 Chair

The committee shall elect a Chair in the same voting manner the Officers are elected. The Chair shall preside over the committee but not vote save for the case of a tie.

4.1.4 Vice Chair

The committee shall elect a Vice Chair in the same voting manner the Officers are elected. The Vice Chair shall preside over the committee in the absence of the Chair and in that role not vote save for the case of a tie. The State from which the Vice Chair is a delegate may appoint another representative to the committee when the Vice Chair is serving as Chair.

4.1.5 Sub-Committees

The committee may divide into sub-committees with fewer members than the committee and shall elect a Chair and Vice Chair in the same manner as the committee. The Chair of the committee shall choose to either be a voting member of a sub-committee or be a non-voting ex-officio member of all sub-committees with the Chair's State selecting another delegate to be a voting member of a sub-committee.

4.2 Amendment Committee

After the initial session of the Convention, the Amendment Committee shall organize.

4.2.1 Purpose of the Committee

The committee shall prepare proposed amendment language which shall be transmitted to the Convention for its consideration and debate. Any amendment language to be presented to the Convention by a State for its consideration by the Convention must originate in the committee. After this committee transmits its report (recommended amendment language) to the Convention, the committee shall not meet unless directed by the Convention. The Convention may amend the report of the committee.

4.2.2 Seating and Participation

One delegate has the right to occupy the seat of the State and speak and vote on behalf of the State and the balance of the delegation may be seated in the same location, space provided, and the State may substitute the delegate in the seat of the State at its discretion.

4.2.3 Chair
The committee shall elect a Chair in the same voting manner the Officers are elected. The Chair shall preside over the committee but not vote save for the case of a tie.

4.2.4 Vice Chair
The committee shall elect a Vice Chair in the same voting manner the Officers are elected. The Vice Chair shall preside over the committee in the absence of the Chair and in that role not vote save for the case of a tie. The State from which the Vice Chair is a delegate may appoint another representative to the committee when the Vice Chair is serving as Chair.

4.2.5 Sub-Committees
The committee may divide into sub-committees with fewer members than the committee and shall elect a Chair and Vice Chair in the same manner as the committee. The Chair of the committee shall choose to either be a voting member of a sub-committee or be a non-voting ex-officio member of all sub-committees with the Chair's State selecting another delegate to be a voting member of a sub-committee.

4.2.6 Specific Issues Before the Committee

4.2.6.1 State Participation
After organizing, the first order of business shall be providing each State attending the Convention equal opportunity and time to present to the committee its opinion, findings, and recommendations regarding the language and content of the amendment subject, including specific amendment language. All presentations are subject to Article 1.

4.2.6.2 Expert Testimony
Expert testimony before the committee by those not a participant of the Convention shall be limited to the subject of the Convention and shall be by invitation. The Chair shall determine the experts and may create a sub-committee to recommend such. The committee, by a majority vote, may include additional experts.

4.3 Credentials Committee

4.3.1 Purpose of the Committee
The committee shall verify the credentials of the delegations after the Opening Session and settle disputes regarding credentials. The decision of the committee may be appealed to the Convention.

4.3.2 Composition
The committee shall be comprised of the elected officers of the Convention and the Chairs of the Rules and Amendment Committees. Each may appoint a substitute to attend a committee meeting. The committee shall select a member to serve as Chair.

4.3.3 State Resolutions
The primary source of verification of the credentials of a delegation shall be the resolution passed by the legislature of the State determining how the delegation should be chosen.

4.3.4 Recall Authority of the States
The committee shall recognize and respect the authority of a State to recall and reappoint members of its delegation pursuant to the resolution approved by their legislature when it appointed its delegation.

4.4 Additional Committees
Additional committees may be created by a majority vote of the Convention provided the committee's function does not create a new rule for the Convention and if so, approval shall be first received from the committee on Rules. If the committee is comprised of delegates, no committee shall have more than one delegate from the same State.

4.5 Committee Debate
The method of participation in committee debate shall be the same method as used in general session.

ARTICLE 5 – Sessions of the Convention

5.1. Composition
The Convention shall be composed of the States from which the legislature has sent a delegation. Recognition by the presiding officer shall be the name of the State and may additionally recognize the individual by name.

5.2 Rules and Procedures
Sessions of the Convention shall be governed by the rules of the Convention and when silent, the rules of parliamentary practice as stated in Mason's Manual of Legislative Procedure, current edition at the time of the Convention.

5.3 Seating and Participation
One delegate has the right to occupy the seat of the State and speak and vote on behalf of the State and the balance of the delegation may be seated in the same location, space provided, and the State may substitute the delegate in the seat of the State at its discretion.

5.4 Sessions

5.4.1 Time of Meeting and Procedure
The Convention shall meet at 9:00 a.m. unless otherwise ordered by the Convention.

5.4.2 Reading of the Journal
Immediately after the President or presiding officer shall have taken the chair and the States in their seats, the journal of the preceding day shall be read by the Secretary unless dispensed with by the consent of the Convention.

5.4.3 Order of Business
At meetings of the Convention, the order of business shall be as follows:
       1. Call Convention to Order
       2. Prayer by an individual approved by the President.
       3. Pledge
       4. Roll Call.
       5. Reading of the Journal.

6. Presentation of petitions, memorials, and remonstrances.

7. Reports of committees.

8. Introduction and first reading of proposals.

9. Reference of proposals.

10. Motions and resolutions.

11. Orders of the day.

12. Committee notices.

5.4.4 Prohibitions on the actions of the Convention

5.4.4.1 Amending Convention Rules

The Convention shall not amend the rules of the Convention until after the Rules Committee has submitted its initial recommendation to the Convention.

5.4.4.2 Proposing and Amending Amendment Language

The Convention will not directly propose for debate specific amendment language until after the Amendment Committee has submitted its initial recommendation to the Convention.

5.4.5 Voting Process

5.4.5.1 Name of the State

Voting shall be in the name of the State without disclosure of the delegation's internal results. After the official tally of the vote, any State may rise and present for the record the internal vote tally of its delegation.

5.4.5.2 Votes Cast

Votes shall be cast as Aye, Nay, Divided, or Pass. If a State passes and does not eventually vote, the State shall not be considered as voting. If a State votes "Divided," the State indicates that the State's delegation is divided and is unable to cast an Aye or Nay vote.

5.4.5.3 Request for Leave

Prior to any vote, a State may ask for time to consult with its delegation on the issue. The request is not debatable and shall be granted by the presiding officer with the period of the leave determined by the presiding officer.

5.4.6 Additional Rules of Procedure

5.4.6.1 Every State, rising to speak, shall address the President or presiding officer; and while the State shall be speaking no one shall pass between them.

5.4.6.2 Of two States rising to speak at the same time, the President or presiding officer shall name the one who shall first be heard.

5.4.6.3 A motion made and seconded, shall be repeated; and if written, as it shall be when any member shall so require, shall be read aloud by the Secretary or transmitted to each delegate's pre-designated electronic device before it shall be debated. No motion, other than a procedural motion, shall be in order unless germane to both the subject matter specified in the State applications on which Congress called the Convention and to 3 the subject matter specified in the Convention call.

5.4.6.4 A motion may be withdrawn at any time before the vote upon it shall have 5 commenced.

5.4.6.5 When a debate shall arise upon a question, no motion, other than to amend the question, to commit it, or to postpone the debate, shall be received.

5.4.6.6 A question that consists of one or more propositions shall, at the request of any State, be divided and put separately as to each proposition.

5.4.6.7 A motion to reconsider a matter that has been determined by a majority may be made, with leave unanimously given, on the same day on which the vote passed; but otherwise not without one day's previous notice; in which last case, if the Convention agree to the reconsideration, the Convention or, by the Convention's leave, the President or presiding officer shall assign a future day for the purpose.

5.4.6.8 A delegate may be called to order by another delegate, as well as by the President or presiding officer, and may be allowed to explain his or her conduct or any expressions supposed to be reprehensible.

5.4.6.9 All questions of order shall be decided by the President or presiding officer, subject to appeal to the Convention, but without debate.

5.4.6.10 Upon a question to recess for the day, which may be made at any time, if it be seconded, the question shall be put without debate.

5.4.6.11 No delegate shall be absent from the Convention, so as to interrupt the representation of his or her State, without leave.

ARTICLE 6 – General and Miscellaneous Provisions

6.1 Costs of the Convention
The costs related to the Convention shall be divided equally among the States attending the Convention and the costs related to the travel, maintenance and provisioning of each State's delegation and staff shall be borne entirely by the State.

6.2 Open Meetings CONVENTION RESOLUTION
Every official session of the Convention including committee and sub-committee meetings shall be held in full view of the public. Every official session of the Convention, including committee and subcommittee meetings, shall be streamed live via a website provided by the Convention and shall be recorded and archived under the direction of the Secretary.

6.3 Adjournment 6 The Convention shall adjourn promptly after completion of the business contained within the call of the Convention.

APPENDIX 5 - RULES OF THE CONSTITUTIONAL CONVENTION

(https://teachingamericanhistory.org/document/the-rules-of-the-convention/)

"A House to do business shall consist of the Deputies of not less than seven States; and all questions shall be decided by the greater number of these which shall be fully represented. But a less number than seven may adjourn from day to day.

"Immediately after the President shall have taken the Chair, and the members their seats, the minutes of the preceding day shall be read by the Secretary.

"Every member, rising to speak, shall address the President; and, while he shall be speaking, none shall pass between them, or hold discourse with another, or read a book, pamphlet, or paper, printed or manuscript. And of two members rising to speak at the same time, the President shall name him who shall be first heard.

"A member shall not speak oftener than twice, without special leave, upon the same question; and not the second time, before every other who had been silent shall have been heard, if he chooses to speak upon the subject.

"A motion, made and seconded, shall be repeated, and, if written, as it shall be when any member shall so require, read aloud, by the Secretary, before it shall be debated; and may be withdrawn at any time before the vote upon it shall have been declared.

"Orders of the day shall be read next after the minutes; and either discussed or postponed, before any other business shall be introduced.

"When a debate shall arise upon a question, no motion, other than to amend the question, to commit it, or to postpone the debate, shall be received.

"A question which is complicated shall, at the request of any member, be divided, and put separately upon the propositions of which it is compounded.

"The determination of a question, although fully debated, shall be postponed, if the Deputies of any State desire it, until the next day.

"A writing which contains any matter brought on to be considered shall be read once throughout, for information; then by paragraphs, to be debated; and again, with the amendments, if any, made on the second reading; and afterwards the question shall be put upon the whole, amended, or approved in its original form, as the case shall be.

"Committees shall be appointed by ballot; and the members who have the greatest number of ballots, although not a majority of the votes present, shall be the Committee. When two or more members have an equal number of votes, the member standing first on the list, in the order of taking down the ballots, shall be preferred.

"A member may be called to order by any other member, as well as by the President; and may be allowed to explain his conduct, or expressions, supposed to be reprehensible. And all questions of order shall be decided by the President, without appeal or debate.

"Upon a question to adjourn, for the day, which may be made at any time, if it be seconded, the question shall be put without a debate.

"When the House shall adjourn, every member shall stand in his place until the President passes him."

"That no member be absent from the House, so as to interrupt the representation of the State, without leave.

"That Committees do not sit whilst the House shall be, or ought to be, sitting.

"That no copy be taken of any entry on the Journal, during the sitting of the House, without leave of the House.

"That members only be permitted to inspect the Journal.

"That nothing spoken in the House be printed, or otherwise published, or communicated, without leave.

"That a motion to reconsider a matter which has been determined by a majority, may be made, with leave, unanimously given, on the same day on which the vote passed; but otherwise, not without one day's previous notice; in which last case, if the House agree to the reconsideration, some future day shall be assigned for that purpose."

CONGREGATIONAL RECORD REFERENCE LIST

- 40 Cong. Rec. 4551 (1906)
- 45 Cong. Rec. 7115, (1910)
- *60 Cong. Rec. 31 (1920)*
- *84 Cong. Rec. 3320 (1939)*
- 89 Cong. Rec. 7523-24, (1943)
- *98 Cong. Rec. 8542 (1952)*
- *98 U.S. 145, Reynolds v. United States, US Supreme Court, 1879*
- *103 Cong. Rec. 6475-76 (1957)*
- *105 Cong. Rec. 3085-86 (1959)*
- *106 Cong. Rec. 14,401 (1960)*
- *106 Cong. Rec. 10,749 (1960)*
- *108 Cong. Rec. 5051, (1962)*
- *109 Cong. Rec. 3788 (1963)*
- *109 Cong. Rec. 2769, 2281, 2769, 5968, 3854, 9942, 1172-73, 10441-42, 14639, 5867, 4779 (1963)*
- *121 Cong. Rec. 12,867 (1975)*
- *125 Cong. Rec. 12,287 (1979)*
- *134 Cong. Rec. 15,363 (1988)*
- *158 Cong. Rec. H3805 (daily ed. May 31, 2011)*
- Cong. Globe, 36th Cong., 2d Sess. 751 (S., Feb. 5, 1861)
- *Cong. Globe, 36th Cong., 2d Sess. 680, (S., Feb. 1,1861)*
- *Cong. Globe, 37th Cong., Special Sess. 1465-66 (S., Mar. 18, 1861)*
- *(H.R. Jour., 1st Cong., 1st Sess. 29-30 (May 6, 1789))*
- *September 4, 1929 Cong. Rec. Vol 71, p. 3369 ("Senate Joint Resolution 65")*
- *September 23, 1929 Cong. Rec. Vol 71, p. 3856 ("Senate Joint Resolution 83")*

REFERENCES

Article V Information Center A Project of the Independence Institute. (n.d.)
Retrieved from
http://articlevinfocenter.com/wp-content/uploads/2021/03/QA.doc-final.pdf

Convention of States, (n.d.) Retrieved from
https://conventionofstates.com/files/model-convention-of-states-application/download

Donnelly, C., (2022, October 14). What Is a Convention of States?. Civics &
Citizenship. Retrieved from
http://articlevinfocenter.com/wp-content/uploads/2021/03/QA.doc-final.pdf

Glass, A., (2016, December 1). House member seeks to abolish the Senate,
April 27, 1911. Retrieved from Politco.
https://www.politico.com/story/2016/04/house-member-seeks-to-abolish-the-senate-april-27-1911-222359

Gordon, L, (1787, December 18). "The Dissent of the Minority of the Convention
of Pennsylvania". Teaching American History. From Retrieved from
https://teachingamericanhistory.org/document/the-dissent-of-the-minority-of-the-convention-of-pennsylvania/

Jones, K. (2017, October 31). A Convention of States Explained. American
Legislative Exchange Council. Retrieved from
https://alec.org/article/a-convention-of-states-explained/

Kaminiski, G. J et al., (2009). The Documentary History of the Ratification of the
Constitution Digital Edition, Retrieved from *https://csac.history.wisc.edu/wp-content/uploads/sites/281/2017/07/delegate_inst1.pdf* - Original source:
Constitutional Documents and Records, 1776-1787, Volume I:
Constitutional Documents and Records, 1776-1787

Laws of the State of Illinois. (1861). Joint Resolutions, *1861 Ill. Laws 281-82.*
Internet Archive. Retrieved from
https://archive.org/details/lawsofstateofill1861illi/page/280/mode/2up

Natelson, R. (2021, March 4). How a 'Convention of States' really works.
Independence Institute.org. Retrieved from
https://i2i.org/how-a-convention-of-states-really works/

Oswald, E, (1787). Image 1 of The Address and reasons of dissent of the minority of the convention, of the state of Pennsylvania, to their constituents. Retrieved from *https://www.loc.gov/resource/bdsdcc.c0401/*

Paulsen, M. (1993). A General Theory of Article V: The Constitutional Lessons of the Twenty-seventh Amendment, The Yale Law Journal, 103(677). Retrieved from https://openyls.law.yale.edu/bitstream/handle/20.500. 13051/8800/32_103YaleLJ677_December1993_.pdf?sequence=2 &isAllowed=y.

Schlafly, Phyllis. (June, 1988) [Supreme Court of the United States letter]. Retrieved from *https://www.phyllisschlafly.com/wp-content/uploads /2020/02/Con-Con-Article-V-Warren-Burger-letter.pdf*

The Article V. Library *(A Public Resource for Articles)* *http://articlevlibrary.com/applications.htm*

Tokayer, M., (2022, February 10). Convention of States - What is it and why it's important: A mechanism unique to the U.S., for taking power from the federal government and giving it back to the people. Frontline News. Retrieved from *https://www.frontline.news/post/convention-of-states-what-is-it-and-why-its-important*

Van Alstyne, William W., (2014, December 9). Does Article V Restrict the States to Calling Unlimited Conventions Only? - A Letter to a Colleague" (1978). Duke University School of Law, Vol. January, 6; William & Mary Law School Research Paper, 9(202). Retrieved from *http://scholarship.law.wm.edu/facpubs/803*

Wikipedia The Free Encyclopedia. (2023, November 15). Original Source from Memorandum to William Carmichael as quoted on page 206 of Valdes, Pinochet's Economists. Retrieved from *https://en.wikipedia.org/wiki/Walter_Heller#cite_ref-6*

Worsnop, R. L. (1964, December 23). Federal-state revenue sharing. Editorial research reports 1964 (Vol. II). CQ Researcher Press. Retrieved from *http://library.cqpress.com/cqresearcher/cqresrre1964122300* *U.S. Supreme Court: Griswold v. Connecticut, 381 U.S. 479 (1965)* U.S. Supreme Court: Roe v. Wade 410 U.S. 113 (1973)